BEYOND NATO

THE MARSHALL PAPER SERIES

After World War II, Brookings scholars played an instru-
mental role in helping the United States craft a concept of
international order and build a set of supporting institutions, including what became known as the Marshall Plan,
in honor of Secretary of State George C. Marshall who spear-
headed the effort. Now, a generation later, the Brookings
Foreign Policy program has evoked that vital historical juncture by launching The Marshall Papers, a new book series
and part of the Order from Chaos project. These short books
will provide accessible research on critical international
questions designed to stimulate debate about how the United
States and others should act to promote an international
order that continues to foster peace, prosperity, and justice.

THE MARSHALL PAPERS

BEYOND NATO

A NEW SECURITY ARCHITECTURE
FOR EASTERN EUROPE

MICHAEL E. O'HANLON

BROOKINGS INSTITUTION PRESS

Washington, D.C.

The Brookings Institution is a private nonprofit organization devoted to research, education, and publication on important issues of domestic and foreign policy. Its principal purpose is to bring the highest quality independent
research and analysis to bear on current and emerging policy problems. Interpretations or conclusions in Brookings publications should be understood
to be solely those of the authors.

Library of Congress Cataloging-in-Publication data are available.
ISBN 9-780-8157-3257-0 (pbk: alk. paper)
ISBN 9-780-8157-3258-7 (ebook)

9 8 7 6 5 4 3 2 1

Typeset in Minion

Composition by Westchester Publishing Services

In memory of Brookings colleagues

Contents

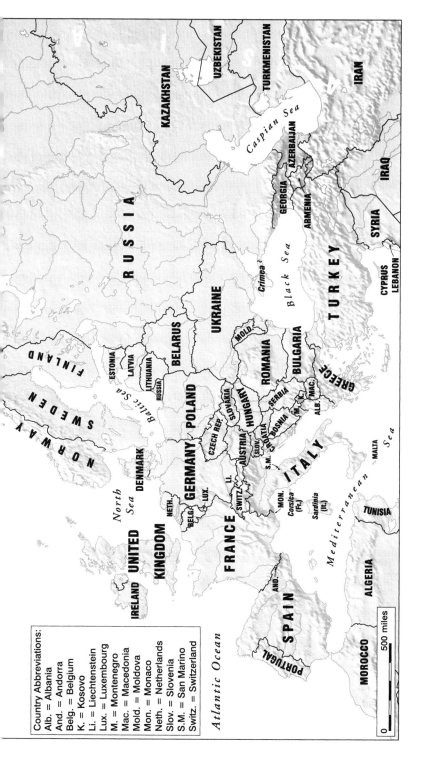

BEYOND NATO

Introduction and Synopsis

Should the North Atlantic Treaty Organization continue to expand? An alliance of just twelve countries when it was created in 1949, NATO grew to sixteen members by the end of the Cold War, and has added another thirteen countries since then. This extremely successful security organization protected Europe in the Cold War, came to America's defense after the 9/11 attacks, and then deployed a major mission to Afghanistan that continues to this day, among numerous other achievements. It has also helped new member states avoid conflict with each other, as with Greece and Turkey during much of the Cold War, and then consolidate democratic rule and civilian control of the armed forces during the period of post–Cold War expansion. It has also become a controversial organization in recent decades, with Russia increasingly objecting to its eastward growth. Great controversy and uncertainty now exist over whether it should someday expand to include not just the Baltic states, which joined in 2004, but other post-Soviet republics, as well, notably Ukraine and Georgia.

This history sets the context for an extremely important issue in U.S. foreign policy today. If the Trump administration is serious about its worthy goal of improving U.S. relations with Russia, how exactly can it do so? After all, Mr. Trump's two immediate predecessors had similar hopes for a better rapport with Putin; both failed. President Trump himself is already using far tougher words toward Russia than he did as a candidate, and his national security team is generally hawkish toward the Putin regime in Moscow. Russia's meddling in America's 2016 elections further mars the situation.

Vladimir Putin and many of those around him are hard-edged autocrats, and there will likely be no easy way to put U.S.-Russian relations fully back on track as long as they are in power. But it may be possible to reduce the risks of rivalry and war by focusing on what may be, in Putin's mind, the fundamental cause of the problem: NATO expansion. We do not owe the Russian strongman any apologies for the enlargement of the twenty-nine-member North Atlantic Treaty Organization to date. Nor should we abandon democratic friends like Ukraine and Georgia to Russian domination. However, there is likely a better way to help them than the current U.S.-led approach.

At present, we have, arguably, created the worst of all worlds. At its 2008 summit, NATO promised eventual membership to Ukraine and Georgia, but it did so without offering any specificity as to when or how that might happen. For now, these two countries, as well as other eastern European neutral states, get no protection from NATO. Knowing of our eventual interest in bringing these nations into an alliance that he sees as adversarial, Vladimir Putin has every incentive to keep them weak and unstable so they will not become eligible for NATO membership. Ukrainian president Petro Poroshenko has been considering a domestic referendum on possible NATO membership; this further fuels the flames. We have inadvertently built a type of NATO-membership doomsday machine that raises the likelihood of conflict in Europe.

It is time that Western nations seek to negotiate a new security architecture for those neutral countries in Eastern Europe today. The core concept would be one of permanent neutrality—at least in the formal sense of ruling out membership in a mutual-defense alliance, most notably NATO. The countries in question collectively make a broken-up arc from Europe's far north to its south—Finland and Sweden; Ukraine and Moldova and Belarus; Georgia and Armenia and Azerbaijan; and finally Cyprus plus Serbia, as well as possibly other Balkan states. The discussion process should begin within NATO, and then include the neutral countries themselves; formal negotiations could then take place with Russia.

The new security architecture would require that Russia, like NATO, commit to help uphold the security of Ukraine, Georgia, Moldova, and other states in the region. Russia would have to withdraw its troops from those countries in a verifiable manner; after that occurred, corresponding sanctions would be lifted. The neutral countries would retain their rights to participate in multilateral security operations on a scale comparable to what has been the case in the past, even those operations that might be led by NATO. They could think of themselves and describe themselves as Western states (or anything else, for that matter). They would have complete sovereignty and self-determination in every sense of the word. But NATO would decide not to invite them into the alliance as members; ideally, they would endorse and promote this concept themselves as a more practical way to ensure their security than the current situation or any other plausible alternative.

Ideally, this architecture might be codified in treaty form and ratified by key legislative bodies, including, in the case of the United States, the U.S. Senate. It should be couched as of indefinite duration. If, someday, the world were to evolve to where a new security order also including Russia were possible, or if Russian politics and strategic culture evolved to the point where Moscow no longer objected, NATO (or a new organization) might expand further, but only after mutual agreement had been reached.

It is worth underscoring that the new security order would guarantee neutral states the right to choose their own form of government, political leadership, diplomatic relations, and economic associations. Notably, Russia would acknowledge the prerogative of those not yet in the European Union (EU) to join the EU (except for its security-related pledges), should that someday be of interest to them as well as current EU members.

To be sure, the concept of neutrality has not always worked out so well historically, as with the fates of Belgium and Holland in the world wars. In other cases, however, such as Switzerland and Austria, it has helped ensure the sovereignty of the neutral nations while also contributing to a more stable security environment in bordering regions.

NATO must not be weakened under the new paradigm. It has been, and remains, a remarkable organization. It did much to protect the security of democratic states and to preserve peace in Europe during the Cold War. It then successfully changed into a mechanism for stabilizing the post–Cold War European order thereafter, including in places such as Bosnia and, more recently, even distant Afghanistan. It also helped several former Warsaw Pact states and the Baltic states solidify their transition to post-communist polities.

NATO has worked hard on its relationship with Russia since the Cold War. It agreed not to station significant foreign combat forces on the territory of any of its members admitted since the Cold War ended. It also created mechanisms such as the North Atlantic Cooperation Council, the Partnership for Peace program, and the NATO-Russia Council to reach out in collegial and collaborative ways to Russia and other former members of the Warsaw Pact.

Yet this is an American, and Western, perspective. Russians in general do not share it. Whether most truly see NATO as a physical threat is a question, but many do see it as an insult—a psychologically and politically imposing former enemy that has approached right up to their border. Russia's declining population and weak economy when contrasted with those of NATO states—roughly a $1.5 trillion GDP and less than 150 million people, versus a combined NATO total of $40 trillion with 900 million people—contribute further to Russia's negative view of NATO. This critical attitude is found not only among Russia's current president and older former Soviet apparatchiks, as well as Mikhail Gorbachev, the father of *glasnost* and *perestroika*, but even among many younger reformers. Putin's sky-high popularity at home, partly a result of his crackdown on critics and competitors, is, nonetheless, also an indication of how strong anti-NATO sentiments have become in Russia.

While pursuing a new security architecture for the neutral states of Eastern Europe, NATO should stay strong and resolute in defense of existing members. The alliance is now stationing a total of some 5,000 troops—a modest force, more of a tripwire than a forward defense—in the Baltic states and Poland. Mr. Trump should signal his intention of sustaining

America's so-called European Reassurance Initiative even as he seeks to negotiate the new security system.

There is no guarantee, of course, that President Putin will prove interested in this idea. Putin may feel he is in an advantageous position to continue to try to weaken NATO, and the EU more generally, by stoking various conflicts, promoting and supporting extremist leaders in Western Europe, fomenting dissent in American politics, and generally keeping the major democratic powers guessing as to what will happen next. He may further conclude that the sanctions imposed on Russia over the Crimea and Donbas aggressions in Ukraine will weaken or dissipate, without any Russian action being necessary, as political forces and leaders change in the West. Putin may also welcome an ongoing standoff with the West for the additional excuses it provides him for his strongman behavior at home and his aggressiveness abroad.

The outcome of any effort to create a new security architecture is, therefore of course, uncertain but it should be attempted, nonetheless. Western leaders should pursue this path confidently and unapologetically, and not portray it as an admission of previous wrongdoing. If Russia refuses to negotiate in good faith, or fails to live up to any deal it might initially support, little will be lost and options for a toughening of future policy against Russia will remain. Indeed, a range of such responses should be developed in advance, including the possibility of expediting consideration of NATO membership for neutral states that are subsequently coerced or attacked by Russia. The hope, of course, is to avoid that. The current strategic situation involving most of the world's great economies and several of its nuclear-weapons states in Europe is quite dangerous, and it will not become less dangerous if simply left on autopilot.

CHAPTER 1

How We Got Here

It is hard to believe, but a quarter century after the fall of the Berlin Wall, the United States and Russia again became adversaries. They remain in such a state today. They may not be military enemies, but their respective military establishments now focus largely on each other in modernizing their weapons and devising force posture plans. Some Russians talk openly of already being at war with the United States; a former deputy supreme allied commander in Europe recently wrote a novel about a war pitting NATO against Russia that he intended as a clarion call about something that really could happen. The Chairman of the Joint Chiefs of Staff in the United States, General Joseph Dunford, testified to Congress in the summer of 2015 that Russia could be America's most dangerous security worry in the world. Dunford subsequently placed Russia among his top concerns when devising his "4 + 1" threat framework—with Russia listed along with North Korea, Iran, China, and ISIS/Salafism/violent extremism as the priority concerns of the Department of Defense. President Donald Trump's early aspirations to put the U.S.-Russia relationship on friendlier footing already appeared to be dashed by the spring of 2017. Russian attacks on Ukraine, a country whose sovereignty the United States as well as Russia and the United Kingdom pledged to help guarantee in the 1994 Budapest Memorandum, have destabilized Europe.

Russian cyber transgressions against Estonia, and provocative military maneuvers near the territories or military assets of various NATO nations, have further underscored that direct military confrontation pitting the United States and allies against the Russian Federation is far from inconceivable. Indeed, Russian aircraft maneuvers near NATO territory or military assets produced up to a doubling in the frequency of NATO fighter "scrambles" designed to intercept the offending aircraft in 2016; serious problems persist today.[1] A Russian concept of "escalate to de-escalate"—purportedly an effective war-winning strategy for any future conflict against the West—has again raised the prominence of nuclear weapons, and veiled nuclear threats, in the Russia-NATO relationship.[2]

How did we get here? And what can we do about it? This short book begins with the first question, the main subject of this chapter, but focuses its main analytical thrust on the second question. Without claiming that the dramatic deterioration in the U.S.-Russian relationship has any single cause, or that any one change in policy can right it, I nonetheless propose a new security architecture for the currently independent states of eastern Europe–Finland and Sweden, George and Ukraine, Moldova and Belarus, Armenia and Azerbaijan, as well as Cyprus and Serbia (and perhaps other currently neutral Balkan countries, as well). I believe this security construct could significantly defuse the acute crisis and dangers in the U.S.-Russian relationship today. A negotiated agreement should be pursued between NATO nations, Russia, and the neutral countries after intensive consultations between NATO states and the neutral states. The goal would be to create a permanently nonaligned zone in eastern Europe while guaranteeing the full diplomatic and economic sovereignty and territorial security of these same countries.

Because the Trump administration, the intended electoral beneficiary of Russian meddling in the 2016 American presidential election, could be the lead player on proposing this new framework, it is especially important to explain why it would not be a concession to Russia or its strongman president. In fact, it would not be a gift to Russia at all.[3] The security architecture would place stringent demands on Russia to keep its hands off the neutral countries and insist it reach fair agreements on existing territorial disputes (otherwise, sanctions could not be lifted and the overall architecture could not be implemented). It would be explicitly understood, and stated, that any subsequent violation of these and other terms could end the entire accord and revive the possibility that some of the countries at issue would join NATO.

Those who might be quick to criticize my proposal should ask if they can really defend the status quo. As of today, NATO has promised Ukraine and Georgia future membership without offering any timetable to that membership or any interim protection—a perfect formula to stoke Russian meddling in those countries and, undoubtedly, an incentive to Moscow to perpetuate the ongoing Russia-Ukraine war. Current policy has failed by leaving NATO half pregnant with membership for Ukraine and Georgia, and Russia incensed over the situation. Whatever the merits of NATO expansion may have been to date—and, as later discussed, there were respectable arguments in its favor (even if not completely convincing ones)—the project has run its course. Indeed, it has become counterproductive.

THE HEADY DAYS OF THE EARLY 1990s, AND ANTECEDENTS OF PROBLEMS TO COME

The warming in U.S.-Russia relations that culminated in very positive American relationships with Mikhail Gorbachev and Boris Yeltsin in the late 1980s and 1990s took some time to develop. From glasnost and perestroika, to the fall of the Berlin Wall, to the iconic image of Yeltsin facing down Soviet tanks in the summer of 1991 as the USSR collapsed, the process took more than half a decade. By the time Bill Clinton was elected president in the United States, however, it was possible to believe that U.S.-Russia relations after the Cold War could be headed to almost as happy a place as U.S.-Germany and U.S.-Japan relationships after World War II.

Problems began to develop fairly early on, however. By 1994, adding insult to the injury of the Soviet Union's own demise, the Warsaw Treaty Organization had also collapsed; meanwhile, NATO was still going strong. East European countries were approaching Brussels about establishing new security arrangements, and then in January 1994, the NATO alliance created the Partnership for Peace (PfP) program. Its declared purpose was to facilitate military and political cooperation between NATO and former members of the defunct Warsaw Pact. However, it did not take long for many Russians, including key reformers like Anatoly Sobchak and Andrei Kokoshin, to begin to view PfP suspiciously as a pathway to NATO expansion for these countries.[4]

As the 1990s unfolded, officials in the Clinton administration felt pressure to reach out to countries like Poland, but they also wanted to support Yeltsin and avoid creating excessive political problems for him at home. They were often told by the reformers around Yeltsin that NATO enlargement would create serious difficulties for the Yeltsin team from Russian nationalists and Communists, and damage the Kremlin's efforts to pursue a pro-Western foreign policy. Yeltsin himself coined the expression that NATO expansion might augur in "a cold peace."[5]

There were reasonable arguments being voiced in the United States to carry out NATO expansion just the same. Some came from diasporas of countries that had been incorporated into the communist world and Warsaw Pact largely against their will and that saw it as only fitting and proper that they be allowed, in effect, to rejoin the West once the Cold War was over. There were additional voices in favor of using NATO to help these former Warsaw Pact states strengthen their young democracies and civilian control of their militaries. And there were those with a long view of history who worried about a return to an aggressive Russia in the future, irrespective of what policies were followed by the West in the meantime. According to this view, Russia's temporary weakness presented an opportunity that should not be missed.[6] Already by February 1995, in fact, the Clinton administration had announced its national security strategy of "engagement and enlargement," in which it underscored that it had "initiated a process that will lead to NATO's expansion."[7]

Thus in the mid-1990s the Clinton administration pushed ahead with enlargement while also seeking to mitigate Moscow's negative reactions. That proved a difficult task. For many Russians, if NATO was still a military alliance and a mechanism for ensuring collective defense, it must be directed against some country—and the Russian Federation was the obvious target.

TABLE 1-1. *Member States of NATO*

	Year joined
Belgium	1949
Canada	1949
Denmark	1949
France	1949
Iceland	1949
Italy	1949
Luxembourg	1949
Netherlands	1949
Norway	1949
Portugal	1949
United Kingdom	1949
United States	1949
Greece	1952
Turkey	1952
Germany	1955
Spain	1982
Czech Republic	1999
Hungary	1999
Poland	1999
Bulgaria	2004
Estonia	2004
Latvia	2004
Lithuania	2004
Romania	2004
Slovakia	2004
Slovenia	2004
Albania	2009
Croatia	2009
Montenegro	2017

NATO Member Countries (www.nato.int/cps/en/nat
ohq/topics_52044.htm).

Yeltsin won reelection in 1996. From that point forward, the Clinton administration felt less need to hold back. Poland, Hungary, and the Czech Republic were soon put on paths to join NATO and became alliance members in 1999. At the same time, Washington and Moscow tried to keep their own relationship moving forward. Notably, in Paris on May 27, 1997, Yeltsin signed the NATO-Russia Founding Act on Mutual Relations. The Founding Act set out the basic political framework for Russia and the alliance to work together, but the forces pushing the two countries apart were rapidly becoming stronger than those holding them together. Subsequent events included the August 1998 Russian financial collapse, the Kosovo war in the spring of 1999, and Russia's renewed war in Chechnya in the summer of 1999.[8]

KOSOVO

In 1999 NATO went to war for the first time in its history in response to Yugoslav military atrocities against ethnic Albanian civilians in Kosovo, which was still part of both Serbia and Yugoslavia.[9] The war came only two weeks after the alliance had admitted Poland, Hungary, and the Czech Republic. NATO did not secure authority from the United Nations to intervene; NATO warplanes bombed Serbian forces in the field and, increasingly, Belgrade. NATO forces, with American troops in the lead, then moved into Kosovo to secure the territory.

NATO's intervention shook the Russian establishment.[10] As Vladimir Putin put it in his March 18, 2014, speech fifteen years later, no one in Russia could believe that NATO had attacked Yugoslavia: "It was hard to believe, even seeing it with my own eyes, that at the end of the twentieth century, one of Europe's capitals, Belgrade, was under missile attack

for several weeks, and then came the real [military] intervention."[11] Moscow could do little about what happened, and
Russian leaders took the intervention almost personally,
given their longstanding ties to Serbia and their sense of close
kinship with fellow Orthodox Christians there.[12]

NATO justified its operation, of course, as a response to
human suffering at the hands of the very same Slobodan
Milosevic who had torn apart Bosnia earlier in the decade.
However, in Moscow, Russian officials interpreted the inter-
vention as a means of expanding NATO's influence in the
Balkans, not as an effort to deal with a humanitarian crisis.[13]

In June, at the end of the bombing campaign, Russian
forces engaged in a tense standoff with NATO troops in
Kosovo. This came as the Clinton administration tried to
persuade Russia to take part in the Kosovo peacekeeping
force (KFOR). Moscow had agreed to a similar arrangement
a couple of years earlier in Bosnia; Russian troops were
still serving there. But this case proved different. After the
intervention which, as noted, occurred with NATO but not
UN approval, Russia resisted the idea of its forces working for
NATO. Moscow also demanded a decisionmaking role in
KFOR, and U.S. military commanders were concerned that
Russia might attempt to create a "Russian sector" in Kosovo.[14]
While these various matters were being discussed in Moscow, Washington, Brussels, and elsewhere, Russian general
Leonid Ivashov sent a Russian troop contingent from Bosnia
to Kosovo, where it secured the main airport in Kosovo's capital of Pristina. However, Russian forces were isolated and soon
running low on food, water, and fuel. New NATO member
Hungary, along with NATO aspirants Bulgaria and Romania,
refused access to their airspace for Russian planes seeking to
conduct resupply runs. At the same point, supreme allied
commander in Europe General Wesley Clark ordered the

NATO commander in Kosovo, British general Michael Jackson, to send in NATO forces to block the runways at the airport. Jackson refused, telling Clark, "Sir, I'm not starting World War III for you."[15] The British did seal off the roads leading to the airport, but they also provided the beleaguered Russian troops with food and water.[16] The result was not a direct conflict between Russia and NATO, thankfully. But it was another humiliation for Moscow.

During this same period Vladimir Putin was gaining greater power within Russia. Putin had been the head of the Federal Security Service; in 1999 he was promoted to chair the Russian Security Council and gained a key role in managing Russia's relationships with NATO and the United States. The Kosovo war then occurred and became a defining moment in Putin's career, one that influenced him deeply.[17] Within months, he was Russia's acting president.

OF COUNTERTERRORISM, COLOR REVOLUTIONS, AND NATO EXPANSION

For a period of time around the turn of the century and early in the 2000s, it seemed that counterterrorism might unite Moscow and Washington in common cause. After all, the two countries had been cooperating on nuclear security through various global nonproliferation efforts as well as the Nunn-Lugar Cooperative Threat Reduction program, so it seemed natural to think they could work together when a new threat presented itself.

In November 1999 Putin, then prime minister, wrote a *New York Times* op-ed asking the American public for support for Russia's second intervention in Chechnya, which had begun a few months before. He defined the fight as a struggle against terrorism that Americans should understand.

After September 11, 2001, the terrorist strikes on U.S. soil reinforced Putin's view that America and Russia should be united in purpose. Then-President Putin immediately reached out to President George W. Bush to express his sympathy and offer his assistance.[18] Indeed, shortly before the 9/11 attacks, Putin had called Bush to warn him about a terrorist threat that Russian intelligence had identified.[19] Putin expected Washington would see linkages between al Qaeda in Afghanistan and terrorists in Chechnya. He also believed he could help the United States.[20] He expected American sympathy and support for his wars against terrorism, especially in light of the terrible terrorist attacks against Russians that began around 1995 and continued into the first decade of the 2000s and beyond.[21]

That did not happen. Chechnya remained a major subject of contention between Russia and the United States. There was to be no coalition.[22] The United States saw Russia's situation as entirely different from its own. The al Qaeda threat justified a global war on terrorism; America and its allies were under direct and unprovoked assault. By contrast, the Chechnya situation, in Washington's eyes, was an internal conflict. The terrorist acts that emanated from the North Caucasus were directed only against Russian targets. Most Americans felt Russia had largely brought its problems upon itself because of the brutal way it fought the Chechnya campaigns.[23]

After the 9/11 attacks, Putin was befuddled by America. He even blamed himself for not having been sufficiently emphatic in his warnings and his efforts to fashion a unified front against the extremist threat.[24] As time went on, however, he blamed the United States more and more—for being overly assertive in Russia's backyard and the Middle East, yet at the same time inept in how it wielded power. Iraq and Afghanistan and Libya went badly, demonstrating American incompetence in his eyes. Yet Putin also ascribed almost super-human powers to Washington for its purported roles in the Rose, Orange, Tulip, and Maydan revolutions (in Georgia in 2003, Ukraine in 2004–05, Kyrgyzstan in 2005, and Ukraine again in 2013–14, respectively), as well as with the domestic opposition to his own attempt to regain the Russian presidency in 2012. There was apparent contradiction in these contrasting interpretations of America's supposed omnipotence mixed with sheer fecklessness, but there was probably a good deal of sincerity in both aspects of Putin's somewhat oxymoronic view of the United States.

Shortly after the 9/11 attacks, in December 2001, Washington announced it was pulling out of the 1972 Anti-Ballistic Missile (ABM) Treaty and would move ahead with creating a new missile defense system to counter threats from countries like Iraq or North Korea or Iran—the so-called rogue states or "axis of evil." Putin's initial response was relatively muted, perhaps because the 9/11 attacks were still so recent and because both the Putin and Bush presidencies were still in their early, hopeful days. However, in ensuing months and years, many of the old Russian fears about Ronald Reagan's Strategic Defense Initiative, his "Star Wars" program, were gradually resurrected in Moscow. Putin and other Russian officials expressed growing opposition to the system. Putin came to believe, it would appear, that American missile defense was more about diminishing Russia's nuclear deterrent than about countering threats from small, extremist states.[25]

The U.S.-led invasion of Afghanistan was perhaps not so hard for Moscow to stomach. Its eye-for-an-eye character probably made sense to Putin. And the next year, Moscow and NATO established a new NATO-Russia Council at the alliance's Rome summit. NATO leaders saw the creation of this council as yet one more piece of evidence that the West was bending over backward to help Russia, to treat it with respect, and to assuage its worries about post–Cold War security in Europe. On top of that, Western economic help to Russia had been moderately generous since the Cold War had ended. Russia's economic travails continued, of course, but they were, from this viewpoint, the result of the inevitable pain of transforming a command economy into a free-market system combined with some bad behavior by Russian oligarchs who were exploiting their fellow citizens with robber-baron-like activities. The major NATO states were doing all they reasonably could to help, in economic and political and security spheres. At least, that was how the West saw it, and at times Putin did not seem to disagree.

Of course not all was well, and the good vibes would not last. That same NATO summit in May 2002 produced decisions leading to the second major round of alliance enlargement in March 2004, including Bulgaria, Estonia, Latvia, Lithuania, Romania, Slovakia, and Slovenia. From Moscow's perspective, the inclusion of Estonia, Latvia, and Lithuania in the group was particularly galling because they had been part of the Russian Empire and the Soviet Union.[26] The three Baltic states, along with the Czech Republic, Hungary, Poland, Slovakia, and Slovenia, were also admitted to the European Union in May of that same year, and Bulgaria and Romania joined in 2007.

Moreover, the 2003 U.S.-led intervention in Iraq convinced Putin even more that the United States was looking for pretexts to act hegemonically, throwing its military weight around the Mideast region and the world. Indeed, Putin, as well as Russian intelligence, apparently believed that Iraqi leader Saddam Hussein was bluffing about his possession of chemical and other weapons of mass destruction (WMD). They stated this bluntly to U.S. officials on numerous occasions.[27] As the intervention quickly went south later in 2003, Putin's anger at alleged American imperiousness was increasingly combined with disdain for how ineffectually the United States seemed to be employing its power around the world.

When the terrible Beslan school terrorist attack in September 2004 took place in Russia, two years after the bloody Moscow Dubrovka Theater attack, Western reactions to Moscow's response furthered in Putin's mind the idea that a double standard was being applied against Russia.[28] The Orange Revolution in Ukraine in 2004–05 was important in this regard, as well. Putin was always somewhat dismissive of Ukraine as a truly separate and sovereign entity capable of genuinely independent action. Thus, he believed the massive demonstrations in Ukraine known as the Orange Revolution could only have been orchestrated from the outside.[29] The Bush administration's Freedom Agenda and American neo-imperialism more generally were the most likely culprits.[30] Putin did not accept the sincerity of U.S. democracy-promotion efforts. He saw their roots in the Cold War and in Washington's unwillingness to accept the legitimacy of Russia's political system. And now they were affecting a fairly large country that was very close to home for Russia.

Then there was Georgia. The Kremlin was very concerned about U.S. support for the Georgian government of Mikheil Saakashvili as the Bush presidency progressed into its second term.[31] The strengthening relationship between Tbilisi and Washington raised worries about Georgia's eventual membership in NATO. Given Georgia's distance from Europe and the North Atlantic, it was increasingly hard for many Russians to view NATO's interest in Georgian membership as anything more than imperial overstretch, and at their own country's expense.[32]

THINGS FALL APART

Thus the stage was set for a confluence of events in 2007 and 2008 that probably marked the decisive turning point in relations between Vladimir Putin and the West in particular, as Clifford Gaddy and Fiona Hill have persuasively argued. At the February 2007 Munich Security Conference, Putin gave the following public remarks:

> It turns out that NATO has put its frontline forces on our borders, and we continue to strictly fulfill the treaty obligations and do not react to these actions at all. I think it is obvious that NATO expansion does not have any relation with the modernization of the Alliance itself or with ensuring security in Europe. On the contrary, it represents a serious provocation that reduces the level of mutual trust. And we have the right to ask: against whom is this expansion intended?[33]

There was no acknowledgment by Putin that the United States and major Western European NATO states demonstrated restraint by not moving combat power into permanent bases in the alliance's new eastern regions, or that American military energies at the time were clearly focused on Iraq and Afghanistan, not Europe.

A year later, Putin made almost identical remarks to the press on the sidelines of the April 2008 NATO Summit in Bucharest, Romania. On this occasion, building on his remarks in Munich, Putin returned to what he saw as the fundamental questions posed by NATO's continued existence and seemingly inexorable expansion, even after the collapse of the Soviet Union. Putin stated:

It is obvious that today there is no Soviet Union, no eastern bloc and no Warsaw Pact. So NATO exists to confront whom? We hear that it exists in order to solve today's problems and challenges. Which ones? What are the problems and challenges? . . . I think that many here in this room would agree with me that, in itself, the existence of the NATO bloc is not an effective answer to today's challenges and threats. But we recognize that it is nonetheless a factor in today's international life, a factor in international security, and that is why we cooperate with the bloc. With regard to expansion, I heard today that this expansion is not against Russia. You know, I have a great interest in and love for European history, including German history. Bismarck was an important German and European political leader. He said that in such matters what is important is not the intention but the capability. . . . We have withdrawn our troops deployed in eastern Europe, and withdrawn almost all large and heavy weapons from the European part of Russia. And what happened? A base in Romania, where we are now, one in Bulgaria, an American missile defense area in Poland and the Czech Republic. That all means moving military infrastructure to our borders.[34]

In February 2008, the United States and several European states recognized Kosovo against Russia's wishes. That reopened old wounds from 1999 and conjured up the immediate possibility of Kosovo, heretofore a province of Serbia, becoming a NATO member someday. Putin declared this "a harmful and dangerous precedent" and immediately raised the implications of Kosovo's independence for Georgia's secessionist republics of Abkhazia and South Ossetia.[35]

NATO's Bucharest summit in April then promised Georgia and Ukraine eventual membership. The fact that NATO leaders chose not to take the technical step of offering Kiev and Tbilisi formal Membership Action Plans was little solace.

In June 2008 Dmitry Medvedev, just inaugurated as Russian president, gave his first major foreign policy speech abroad. In his speech, he proposed the creation of a new European security arrangement and treaty, an idea that was quickly rejected by the United States and its allies.[36] Even though it was vague, and even though in later revisions it acknowledged NATO's continued right to exist, Medvedev's vision may have come too close to condemning the NATO alliance to obsolescence—or at least to a constrained future role—for the West to accept it.[37]

By August 2008 Russia had gone to war with Georgia. Russia's incursion was justified as a response to President Saakashvili's decision to launch his own attack against separatists in South Ossetia. Georgian shelling killed Russian peacekeepers in the South Ossetian capital Tskhinvali, provoking a full-scale Russian military invasion. But in a broader sense, it was the result of pressures that had been building in Russian minds for many years.[38]

The year 2009 marked the arrival of a new American president and Mr. Obama's "reset" policy with Russia.[39] The approach seemed to address Putin's main demand that Russia be treated with respect and pragmatism on major issues of mutual interest, but it did not succeed. The first year and a half of the Obama presidency produced a New START Treaty, a new architecture for European missile defense, further cooperation on Iran and North Korea sanctions, and the opening of the Northern Distribution Network into Afghanistan—providing NATO with multiple new logistics options that involved Russian territory or other former Soviet republics. However, things soon deteriorated. In Moscow's eyes, the perceived offenses included America's unsuccessful handling of aspects of the Arab Spring, such as the NATO Libya intervention which quickly exceeded the scope of the UN Security Council resolution approving it, to the unsteady American handlings of unrest in Syria and Egypt, to the Sergei Magnitsky Act targeting Russian officials who had been complicit in the death of a Russian human rights lawyer.[40] That tragedy and other Russian crackdowns on dissent at home led to more critical American words concerning Russian internal politics.

A vicious cycle had developed. Putin and his inner circle, probably never true democrats at heart, were critiqued by Washington for their suppression, including through occasional violence, of internal dissent. These critiques enraged Putin, who then saw America's hand in any Russian political activity that did not support him (such as party-building and other democracy-promotion activities), and he clamped down even more forcefully. To maintain Russian public support for his short-circuiting of proper democratic practices, he pointed to a supposedly hostile and devious West that was purportedly inciting Russians to turn against each other. The combination of disinformation and coercion worked, at least at home. In recent years—according to what Russians tell pollsters (whether they feel free in expressing their true views or not is another matter)—Putin's internal popularity has typically been 80 to 90 percent.[41]

In a 2017 interview with the *National Interest*, Russian foreign minister Sergey Lavrov pointed to a speech that Secretary of State Hillary Clinton gave in December 2012 in Ireland in which she expressed the hope that the United States could slow Moscow's efforts to "re-Sovietize the former

Soviet space." One might have thought all could agree that re-Sovietization was not in anyone's interest. Yet Lavrov argued that such words revealed malevolent and expansionist American intent that was manifest even before the crises of Crimea and Ukraine.[42]

On September 11, 2013, on the anniversary of the 9/11 terrorist attacks, Putin again wrote an op-ed in the *New York Times.* Putin was extremely critical of America's style of world leadership. He argued: "It is alarming that military intervention in internal conflicts in foreign countries has become commonplace for the United States. Is it in America's long-term interest? I doubt it. Millions around the world increasingly see America not as a model of democracy but as relying solely on brute force, cobbling coalitions together under the slogan 'you're either with us or against us.' "[43]

The Ukraine crisis of 2013–14 was the nail in the coffin. The precipitating events were not about NATO membership, but Ukraine's general westward movement and consideration of closer ties to the European Union. Yet they were in a broader context in which eventual NATO membership for Ukraine was clearly on the table, admittedly making it hard to disentangle the relative importance of the various factors in Putin's mind. One thing the Russian strongman did clearly believe is that the various color revolutions as well as this latest, the Maydan uprising, were not indigenous or legitimate. Of course, he was bound not to like them; they had the aggregate effect of replacing pro-Moscow politicians with pro-Western regimes. Worse, Putin saw the hand of the West behind all of them. He blamed Western involvement with new political parties and nongovernmental organizations and other new actors in these young countries for what transpired. Not only was it against his own interests; he saw these developments as bad for the countries themselves.

By this time, Putin could invoke the failed Arab Spring movements in the Middle East to reinforce his argument. The West, Putin argued in a March 2014 speech, tried to impose a set of "standards, which were in no way suitable for either the way of life, or the traditions, or the cultures of these peoples. As a result, instead of democracy and freedom—there was chaos and the outbreak of violence, a series of revolutions. The 'Arab Spring' was replaced by the 'Arab Winter.'"[44] This speech helped justify, for Putin, Russian aggression against Ukraine in Crimea and in the Donbas region, in cyberspace (including with an attack on the electricity grid), and beyond. The West, of course, saw these actions as entirely illegitimate, a threat to basic international order, and proof of Putin's autocratic and strongman ways.[45] Although they did not embark on a major transfer of lethal weaponry, several NATO countries, including the United States, did assist the Ukrainian military in various ways in response to Russia's aggression, further hardening battle lines.[46]

The reset was dead. By the end of the Obama years, so were 10,000 Ukrainians, who perished in civil war, as well as 300 passengers on a Malaysian jet shot down by a Russian anti-aircraft missile.

The breakdown in relations extended to the Middle East, too. While the West blamed Putin for bloody, brutal Russian tactics in Syria from 2015 onward that primarily killed moderate insurgents (rather than the purported ISIS targets), Putin saw that war as another demonstration of the West's naiveté about power politics and under-appreciation for the importance of political stability in troubled countries.[47]

In short, a quarter century after the end of the Cold War, NATO and Russia had again effectively become adversaries.

ECONOMIC AND MILITARY POWER

Two more dimensions of the equation need to be overlaid with this brief review of security events and crises: trends in economics and trends in the related matter of military spending and defense modernization.

During Yeltsin's time in power, Russia's economic power and the standard of living of its people deteriorated precipitously. Western observers often forget how much Gorbachev and Yeltsin, seen as reformers and democrats in much of NATO, are generally associated with the decline of the state by Russian citizens.

Putin changed that. He presided over a stabilization of the Russian economy. To be sure, the economy remained unhealthy in many ways, and it remained dwarfed by NATO's aggregate wealth. But at least it ceased its free fall in the 2000s, benefiting from, among other things, the rise in many commodity prices on global markets. As Gaddy and Hill have emphasized, Russia's capacities for action changed dramatically in the summer of 2006, when Moscow finally paid off the last of its international debt to the so-called Paris Club of major creditor nations. Putin had also paid off Russia's debt to the International Monetary Fund by then. Russia was effectively unchained from its financial shackles to foreign countries and international financial institutions. The United States and the West could no longer exert pressure over Russia using debt and the prospect of new loans in the way they had since the Cold War ended.[48]

The global financial crisis and great recession of 2008 and onward caused less damage to Russia than to some Western states, and perhaps, therefore, taught Putin and fellow Russians another strategic lesson: there was value to a degree of autarky and independence. When sanctions were

TABLE 1-2. *Population and Gross Domestic Product for Key Countries*

Country	Population (millions)	GDP (US$ billions, 2016)
NATO		
Albania	3.0	12.1
Belgium	11.4	470.0
Bulgaria	7.1	50.4
Canada	35.4	1,530.0
Croatia	4.3	49.9
Czech Republic	10.7	194.0
Denmark	5.6	303.0
Estonia	1.3	23.5
France	66.8	2,490.0
Germany	80.7	3,490.0
Greece	10.8	196.0
Hungary	9.9	117.0
Iceland	0.4	19.4
Italy	62.0	1,850.0
Latvia	2.0	27.9
Lithuania	2.8	42.8
Luxembourg	0.6	61.0
Montenegro	0.6	4.2
Netherlands	17.0	770.0
Norway	5.3	376.0
Poland	38.5	467.0
Portugal	10.8	206.0
Romania	21.6	187.0
Slovakia	5.5	90.3
Slovenia	2.0	44.1
Spain	48.6	1,250.0
Turkey	80.3	736.0
United Kingdom	64.4	2,650.0
United States	324.0	18,600.0
Total	*933.4*	*36,307.6*

(continued)

TABLE 1-2. *(continued)*

Country	Population (millions)	GDP (US$ billions, 2016)
RUSSIA		
Russia	142.4	1,270.0
Total	*142.4*	*1,270.0*
NEUTRAL AND CSTO		
Armenia	3.1	10.8
Azerbaijan	9.9	35.7
Belarus	9.6	48.1
Bosnia-Herzegovina	3.9	16.5
Cyprus	1.2	19.9
Finland	5.5	239.0
Georgia	4.9	14.5
Kosovo*	1.8	6.6
Macedonia	2.1	10.5
Moldova	3.5	6.7
Serbia	7.1	37.8
Sweden	9.9	517.0
Ukraine	44.2	87.2
Total	*106.7*	*919.3*
OTHER NEUTRAL		
Austria	8.7	387.0
Ireland	4.9	308.0
Malta	0.4	10.5
Switzerland	8.2	662.0
Total	*22.2*	*1,367.5*

*Kosovo's independence is not yet fully established.

Source: International Institute for Strategic Studies, *The Military Balance 2017* (New York: Routledge Press, 2017), pp. 42, 45, 90, 91, 93, 96, 98, 100, 102, 104, 106, 108, 110, 116, 120, 123, 125, 127, 131, 135, 137, 139, 142, 144, 149, 152, 154, 156, 158, 161, 164, 166, 170, 199, 200, 203, 205, 209, 210.

The World Fact Book, "Kosovo," Central Intelligence Agency, March 14, 2017 (www.cia.gov/library/publications/the-world-factbook/geos/kv.html).

applied by the West after the Crimea and Donbas operations in Ukraine, Putin may not have welcomed the punishment, but he, perhaps, saw a silver lining in helping ensure that Russia would be reminded to take care of itself and not depend on the outside world for its economic viability.

Russia's economic recovery also permitted a reassertion of military power. Since the collapse of the Soviet Union, Russia's armed forces had been the target of a series of largely ineffectual reform programs. They were also far less well resourced than NATO's forces. However, in late 2008, after the difficult war with Georgia, Russia launched a much more serious set of reforms under Defense Minister Anatoliy Serdyukov.[49] The general improvement in Russia's economy and desires for a reassertion of national power led to an expansion in available resources to fund the country's armed forces and implement those reforms.

The modernization agenda had several components. A central goal was to create higher-performance, more mobile, and better-equipped units. The military was shrunk by about a third, and officer ranks were reduced by half. As with the U.S. military in this time period, the main unit of ground combat capability was reduced from the division to the brigade, and remaining brigades were more fully staffed and manned. Most tanks were eliminated as well, though some 2,000 remained out of an initial force ten times that size. Military education was revamped; pay was improved; professionalism was emphasized.[50]

In late 2010 then-Prime Minister Putin announced a dramatic weapons procurement plan to go along with this earlier set of reforms in personnel, force structure, and readiness. Ambitiously, some $700 billion was projected for weapons modernization over a ten-year time frame. This plan included a wide range of equipment. For example, in the naval realm it

TABLE 1-3. *Defense Spending and Active Force Size for Key Countries*

Country	GDP on defense (percent)	Defense budget (US$ millions, 2016)	Active force size
NATO			
Albania	0.95	115	8,000
Belgium	0.83	3,900	29,600
Bulgaria	1.35	678	31,300
Canada	0.86	13,200	63,000
Croatia	1.18	588	15,550
Czech Republic	1.02	1,970	21,950
Denmark	1.17	3,550	16,600
Estonia	2.14	503	6,400
France	1.90	47,200	202,950
Germany	1.10	38,300	176,800
Greece	2.37	4,640	142,950
Hungary	0.85	996	26,500
Iceland	0.16	31	250
Italy	1.21	22,300	174,500
Latvia	1.47	411	5,310
Lithuania	1.50	642	17,030
Luxembourg	0.36	220	900
Montenegro	1.63	69	1,950
Netherlands	1.19	9,190	35,410
Norway	1.59	5,970	24,950
Poland	1.94	9,080	99,300
Portugal	1.06	2,180	29,600
Romania	1.49	2,780	70,500
Slovakia	1.09	983	15,850
Slovenia	1.02	450	7,250
Spain	0.98	12,200	123,200
Turkey	1.19	8,760	355,200
United Kingdom	1.98	52,500	152,350
United States	3.25	604,000	1,347,300
Average/Total/Total	*1.34*	*847,300*	*3,200,500*

TABLE 1-3. *(continued)*

Country	GDP on defense (percent)	Defense budget (US$ millions, 2016)	Active force size
RUSSIA			
Russia	3.67	46,600	831,000
Average/Total/Total	*3.67*	*46,600*	*831,000*
NEUTRAL AND CSTO			
Armenia	3.96	428	44,800
Azerbaijan	4.03	1,440	66,950
Belarus	1.06	509	48,000
Bosnia-Herzegovina	1.16	191	10,500
Cyprus	1.79	356	12,000
Finland	1.37	3,280	22,200
Georgia	1.98	287	20,650
Kosovo*	NA	NA	NA
Macedonia	1.02	107	8,000
Moldova	0.44	29	5,150
Serbia	1.34	507	28,150
Sweden	1.13	5,830	29,750
Ukraine	2.49	2,170	204,000
Average/Total/Total	*1.80*	*15,100*	*502,100*
OTHER NEUTRAL			
Austria	0.53	2,070	21,350
Ireland	0.32	1,000	9,100
Malta	0.55	58	1,950
Switzerland	0.71	4,720	20,950
Average/Total/Total	*0.53*	*7,800*	*53,350*

*Kosovo's independence is not yet fully established.
Sources: International Institute for Strategic Studies, *The Military Balance 2017* (New York: Routledge Press, 2017), pp. 42, 45, 90, 91, 93, 96, 98, 100, 102, 104, 106, 108, 110, 116, 120, 123, 125, 127, 131, 135, 137, 139, 142, 144, 149, 152, 154, 156, 158, 161, 164, 166, 170, 199, 200, 203, 205, 209, 210.
The World Fact Book, "Kosovo," Central Intelligence Agency (www.cia.gov /library/publications/the-world-factbook/geos/kv.html).

included Yasen-class nuclear attack submarines, Lada-class and Kilo-class diesel attack subs, several classes of frigates and corvettes, Borey-class ballistic missile submarines, and two Mistral-class amphibious vessels from France.[51] Fighter aircraft deliveries began to average about two dozen a year, including MiG-29SMT, Su-34, and Su-35S jets.[52]

By 2014 annual military spending levels had reached the range of $80 billion, almost double the 2008 figure. The imposition of sanctions against Russia in the course of the Ukraine crisis, followed by the plummeting of global oil prices, changed this plan. But much of its thrust survived. And much of it had been accomplished by 2014, when the Russian military began to truly swing back into action.

CONCLUSION

By 2013, as the crisis in Ukraine began to unfold, Putin's worldview and his view of America had become quite dark. The stage was thus set for the Maydan revolution in Ukraine, and for the sense in Putin's mind that the West orchestrated that revolution to further weaken Moscow. The narrative was strengthened when, having helped negotiate a graceful departure for President Viktor Yanukovych in February 2014, the West seemed to quickly abandon the plan once his ouster could be achieved more quickly. The conditions were in place for the unleashing of "little green men," and much more.

As Putin concluded in his March 18, 2014, speech, after invading and just before annexing Crimea: "Russia strived to engage in dialogue with our colleagues in the West. We constantly propose[d] cooperation on every critical question, [we] want[ed] to strengthen the level of trust, [we] want[ed] our relations to be equal, open and honest. But we did not see reciprocal steps [from the West]." Limited by lack of direct contacts

TABLE 1-4. *Soviet versus Russian Military Indicators a Quarter Century after the Cold War*

	Soviet military 1989	Russian military 2014
Annual estimated budget (2014 $)	$225 billion	$82 billion
Active military personnel	4,250,000	845,000
Reserve personnel	5,560,000	2,000,000
Active-duty army strength	1,600,000	285,000
ICBMs	1,450	356
Bombers	630	220
Fighter aircraft	7,000	1,240
Submarines	368	64
Principal surface combatants	264	33

Sources: International Institute for Strategic Studies, *The Military Balance 1989–1990* (Oxford, England, 1989), pp. 32–37, and *The Military Balance 2014* (Oxfordshire, England, 2014), pp. 180–86.

with the United States and driven by his threat perceptions, Putin believed he had been rebuffed or deceived at every turn by the West. His worldview, and that of many other Russians, may not be persuasive to most Western observers, but it does appear to be largely sincere.

Meanwhile, negative Western views of Russia and Putin have spiked considerably. Russia's aggressions against Ukraine in 2014, which continue to this day, were followed by its support for Syrian president Bashar al-Assad in 2015. Russia's military assertiveness went from relatively limited and short in Georgia in 2008 to quick and decisive in Crimea in early 2014 to sustained and deadly in the Donbas region thereafter—to absolutely brutal in Syria, where its support for the inhumane tactics of Assad's forces have deprived its intervention of any legitimacy whatsoever in Western eyes.

And of course Russian meddling in the American elections of 2016 added insult to injury. Putin saw it, perhaps, as repaying the favor that U.S. democracy-promotion efforts had done him several years earlier. But Americans rejected this comparison. Even Republicans who might have supported a Trump victory could not accept Russian meddling through hacking and disinformation, or view it as somehow simply giving the United States its just deserts.

The advent of the Trump administration in Washington, thus, comes at a crucial moment in history. The odds of Mr. Trump being able to engineer an improvement in relations seem rather low unless he can fundamentally recast relations between the West and Russia that twenty-eight years of post–Cold War history have done so much to undermine.

In the remaining chapters, I explore how a substantial change in U.S.-Russia and NATO-Russia relations might be attempted through the creation of a new security architecture. First, in chapter 2, I review briefly the basic state of national security and national security politics in the key neutral states that are the focal point of the proposal. In chapter 3, I make the case for a new security paradigm or structure for the neutral states of eastern Europe, and in chapter 4, I sketch out the main contours and characteristics of such a plan.

CHAPTER 2

A Primer on Europe's Frontier States Today

Any discussion of a future security architecture for currently neutral states in eastern Europe should be cogni-
zant of the histories, strategic environments, and current
political debates in these key countries. Specialists will
not require this primer, but since the territory in question
stretches all the way from the Nordic region down through
the Balkans and into the Mediterranean, it may be worth
summarizing the basics to establish a common foundation
for the subsequent proposal of a new security system for the
overall area.

The purpose here is not to suggest that each and every
one of the countries at issue should be given a veto over the
proposal. Indeed, the security architecture I propose is simple
and in most ways passive. It is not about creating a new
organization or new obligations for any of these presently
neutral countries, and it would not bar them from teaming
up with each other in various combinations if they so wish.

Nor would it preclude them from self-identifying any way they wished in the future—including as "Western" states. The issue here is simply about formal security alliances involving mutual-defense pacts with major Western powers, most notably NATO.

Regardless, American and NATO values require taking into account the interests and views of these countries, which, ideally, would be part of the consultation and negotiation process before NATO and Russia embarked on that effort. Certainly the case for a new security system will be stronger if those countries that would be most affected believe they would benefit from it and generally support—or at least accept—the concept. It is, thus, essential to have some feel for their security contexts prior to embarking on the design of a new paradigm or architecture. This chapter examines four groups of countries—Sweden and Finland; Ukraine, Georgia, Moldova, and Belarus; Armenia and Azerbaijan; and Cyprus and Serbia—plus other countries in the Balkans.

None of these countries except Ukraine, with 45 million inhabitants, has a large population. Sweden has just under 10 million people and Finland just over 5 million. Georgia has 5 million inhabitants, Belarus 10 million, and Moldova under 4 million. Armenia has 3 million souls and Azerbaijan 10 million. Cyprus has a population just over 1 million and Serbia some 7 million. All told, the ten countries at issue have 90 million citizens, half of them in Ukraine.

In military terms, Sweden is rather impressive for a country with a small population and spends $5 billion a year on its armed forces. Ukraine spends roughly as much; otherwise, only Azerbaijan cracks the $1 billion threshold, at about $1.7 billion annually. Only Ukraine exceeds 100,000 uniformed personnel in its armed forces (in its case, the number is now at least 200,000). Several of the countries deploy a couple hundred troops in various peacekeeping missions around the world; only Georgia approaches the 1,000 figure (which is impressive, given its small size).[1] These countries are important and valuable members of the international community for many reasons, but it is safe to say that they are not strategic or military powerhouses. Their overall importance to the global order probably has, at least at present, much more to do with how they affect broader European security dynamics than with their own direct military contributions, deployments, or operations.

This is not an excuse for Russian domination of these small states in any purported sphere of influence, no matter that some Russians might wish to claim otherwise. Indeed, there is one important theme that emerges from these brief pages that even specialists need to take greater stock of: these are proud, independent, and fully sovereign nations that deserve their own security, prosperity, and self-determination. Even those that were part of a Russian empire at some previous stage in history developed their own strong identities over time. Moreover, those Russian "empires" were often fluid and amorphous constructions, not strong nation-states of the Westphalian variety. The modest sizes and geographic locations of the countries considered here in no way compromise their inherent rights as complete members of the international community, with all the pride associated with true nations and all the prerogatives associated with statehood. They are not tributary states of Russia, or appendages of the Russian empire, or part of some special Russian sphere of influence and interest.

FINLAND AND SWEDEN

The Nordic countries of Finland and Sweden are crucial parts of any discussion about NATO's future, even if they

tend to be somewhat less in the crosshairs of the debate than
Ukraine or Georgia.

Finland and Sweden, two remarkable, market-oriented
democracies, are already Western countries by most defini-
tions. Their political systems, standards of living, and overall
quality of life are akin to those of nations in NATO and the
European Union. They are in these regards more similar to
neutral countries like Austria or Switzerland than to most
other neutral countries of eastern Europe that are the focus of
this book. In addition, while they have modest populations—a
bit more than 5 million for Finland and just under 10 million
for Sweden—they are geographically large. Finland shares a
long border with Russia. Sweden does not directly make contact with Russia, as Norway stretches around, so to speak, and
touches the northern tip of Russia's Kola Peninsula, but Sweden, too, is very close to Russia.

Finland and Sweden are the two Nordic countries not part
of NATO today. (Norway, Denmark, and Iceland are also
Nordic states, all within NATO.) Both Finland and Sweden
are members of the European Union, an organization they
joined in 1995. This EU membership, in principle, gives Finland and Sweden very strong security assurances from other
member states, most of which are, of course, also in NATO.
The absence of an American commitment and the somewhat
murkier character of that European Union security pledge,
however, probably make the EU membership more significant
in diplomatic and economic realms than in security terms
per se. (Similarly, for the Baltic states, NATO membership is
likely a much greater source of security-related reassurance
than EU membership.)[2]

Finland and Sweden are also the only two countries bordering the Baltic Sea, besides Russia itself, that are not in
NATO. That sea is sometimes erroneously viewed as an ex-

tension of the Atlantic Ocean when, in fact, it is much closer to an inland body of water geographically; its only access to outside waters is via the narrow Danish Straits. The Baltic Sea's eastern border is mostly made up of the Baltic states. Russia has a small access point near St. Petersburg, in the Gulf of Finland, the easternmost arm of the Baltic Sea. The Baltic's southern border consists of the Polish littoral, plus Russia's Kaliningrad enclave. The northern borders of the Baltic Sea are made up of the long Finnish and Swedish coastlines, largely along what is called the Gulf of Bothnia, an extension of the Baltic in the northward direction. The Baltic Sea's western border is composed of Germany and Denmark.

This brief review of geography is intended simply to underscore the stakes involved in the future of Finland and Sweden. Historically, the waterways—as well as the Finnish, Swedish, and Danish islands in the Baltic Sea— have been strongly contested during numerous conflicts, including both world wars. Today, the Baltic Fleet is one of Russia's four main navies, with some fifty ships (and 25,000 sailors) stationed in Kaliningrad.[3] The waters of this region are crucial for Russian commerce as well, with crude oil exports and other goods transiting through them. If one thinks in strictly military terms, it is a straightforward matter to see that, since the Baltic region is so crucial for European security, NATO operational plans could benefit greatly by having Sweden and Finland within the alliance.[4]

Historically, Sweden and Finland are joined not only by geographic proximity and Nordic heritage but by politics, too. Finland was part of Sweden until 1809, when it was ceded to Russia, remaining part of the latter until the Bolshevik Revolution. Finland then gained independence but was later caught up intensively in World War II, after first fighting the 1939–40 Winter War against the then–Soviet Union to preserve its independence.[5] Though it lost that war and some territory, Finland managed to retain sovereignty. It did so, subsequently, through the Cold War as well. The pejorative phrase "Finlandization" that came into vogue during the Cold War period wrongly implied greater Russian dominance over Finland than was ever the reality, particularly in domestic policy and governance.

Today Sweden and Finland retain much of their previous predisposition toward neutrality—even as they also nurture strong ties with NATO nations, including the Baltic states. The tradition of neutrality in both countries is strong, dating back at least two centuries, and is grounded largely in the pragmatic desire to avoid implication in the European continent's wars, as well as to avoid provoking Russia.[6] Both countries, with their sparse populations, could face challenges in trying to fend off determined invaders, yet their rugged terrain, rough climates, and geographic isolation have generally made it possible to stay out of others' crosshairs with a little bit of prudence. Despite their commitment to neutrality, there has also been a long tradition of quiet security cooperation with the West, which Sweden, in particular, cultivated during the Cold War. Intelligence sharing, among other things, has been extensive.[7]

To be sure, recent Russian assertiveness and bullying behavior in the Baltic region have caused greater anxiety in Finland and Sweden of late. Frequent violations of airspace and territorial waters, buzzing of ships by aircraft, simulated bombing runs by nuclear-capable aircraft, and other unfriendly actions cause understandable consternation in Stockholm and Helsinki.[8]

Historically, Swedish and Finnish voices in favor of joining NATO were relatively few and far between,[9] but public opinion in both countries is increasingly inclined to favor consideration of a NATO membership option more than was ever the case before. A solid majority is still probably against it in Finland, but in Sweden recent polls have reflected an evenly divided populace on the issue.[10] Indeed, the possibility of pursuing NATO membership is shaping up as a major issue for the 2018 parliamentary elections. It is significant that a bloc of parties favoring membership has been leading in some polls as of early 2017.[11] In Finland, a 2016 government white paper explicitly underscored the importance of not just security collaboration with the United States and NATO, but the possible pursuit of a NATO membership option in the future and the value that such an option could provide, even if ultimately not exercised, for helping Finland deal effectively with a more threatening Russia.[12]

In summary, Finland and especially Sweden lean Westward, but they also have strong traditions of neutrality rooted in pragmatism and a rugged sense of self-reliance. Consideration of NATO membership tends to get an airing only when acute threats from Russia and the absence of alternative reliable means of ensuring national security overcome more historical ways of thinking. Of course, at present those Russian threats feel acute in some Nordic quarters, and NATO membership is being discussed much more than has historically been the case.

GEORGIA, UKRAINE, MOLDOVA, AND BELARUS

The four countries of Georgia, Ukraine, Moldova, and Belarus can be usefully analyzed together. Even though Georgia is closer geographically to Armenia and Azerbaijan, it shares the distinction with Ukraine of having been invaded by Russia in recent years and of having been promised, in 2008, eventual NATO membership. Georgia and Ukraine

can, thus, naturally be considered together. Belarus and Moldova are somewhat less contentious, given the former's geostrategic closeness to Moscow and the latter's smaller size
and greater distance from Russia, but both are in the same
general part of Europe and both could certainly be caught
up in a tug-of-war between NATO and Russia in the future.
Moldova also has a part of its territory, the Transnistria region, populated primarily by Russian speakers and func-
tioning as an autonomous zone of sorts, with Russian troops
on its soil, as well as an economy benefiting from Russian
largesse and probably doing better financially than the rest
of the country.[13]

Georgia is wedged between the Black Sea and beautiful
mountains in the Caucasus region of southwest Asia. Though
populated primarily by a distinct ethnic group known, ap-
propriately enough, as Georgians, it is also very cosmopolitan
and diverse.[14] Historically, it was at the crossroads of competition involving Ottomans, Persians, and, for a time,
Mongols before being incorporated into Russia in the early
nineteenth century. Like Ukraine, it had a brief period of
independence, from 1918 through 1921, before being ab-
sorbed into the Soviet Union. The three non-Georgian parts
of Georgia, known as Abkhazia, Adjara, and South Ossetia,
were accorded special status and autonomy in 1936.

Georgia has a special place in Russian hearts. Not only
were some of Russia's greatest writers, like Tolstoy, taken
with the country, but Stalin, his special police chief Lavrenti
Beria, and former Soviet foreign minister Eduard Shevardnadze all came, originally, from Georgia. Georgia's relationship with Russia has thus been one of closeness but also of
some tension, as the strong Georgian sense of identity combined with the country's small size and geographic distance
from Moscow have created complex dynamics.[15]

Events since the end of the Cold War and the dissolution of the Soviet Union have exacerbated tensions. Fighting and ethnic cleansing ensued after Georgia became independent in the early 1990s. Shevardnadze came back to Tbilisi from Russia in 1992 and became president in 1995. But Mikheil Saakashvili and other strong-willed reformers led movements that increasingly opposed what they saw as the Soviet-like ways and patterns of corruption of the Shevardnadze government. They were supported by American NGOs and groups like the National Democratic Institute and the International Republican Institute, government-funded agencies that were sometimes portrayed as part of a conspiracy to steer Georgian politics in a pro-Western direction. Armed only with flowers, these reformers led a "Rose Revolution" after disputed elections in 2003, and demanded Shevardnadze's resignation, which was secured after troops refused the president's order to disperse protesters. Saakashvili then won a hastily arranged election in January 2004, with 94 percent of the vote. As he then tightened ties to Washington and sought to bring Abkhazia as well as South Ossetia back under Tbilisi's control, relations with Putin deteriorated. On April 3, 2008, at its Bucharest summit, NATO promised Georgia eventual membership, in Article 23 of the summit declaration. That same August, Russia invaded Georgia.[16] It kept large forces in South Ossetia and Abkhazia well after the invasion had technically ended and even after the new Obama administration sought a reset in relations between Moscow and Washington.[17]

It is not difficult to see why Georgia, with its European mores and distinct ethnic group and its location far from Moscow, would aspire to be a part of European institutions. It is also not difficult to see why Russia would consider it a serious affront—if not to its actual physical security, then at least to its sense of self and its history and traditions—that

Georgia be courted by faraway NATO and promised future membership.

Of course the story with Georgia did not end in 2008. Saakashvili lost his own hold on power and, indeed, somewhat bizarrely, relocated to Ukraine, where he has become a politician there. He is now very unpopular in Georgia. Indeed, he may have contributed to his former party's defeat in October 2016 elections at the hands of the Georgian Dream party by suggesting that he might come back to seek office again. The NATO question is now on indefinite hold, though in surveys, the idea of membership has consistently remained relatively favorable among Georgians (with 50 to 65 percent typically approving fully and another 20 percent supporting the idea in more lukewarm fashion since 2008–09).[18] The "frozen conflicts" with the autonomous regions persist unresolved, and relations with Russia remain uncertain. Georgia now has an Association Agreement with the European Union, which surely raises eyebrows and furrows foreheads in Moscow.[19] Even so, the country continues to struggle in many ways, including in the strength of its civil society and democratic institutions, and its economy remains troubled. The Georgian future remains murky.[20]

Ukraine is a case similar to Georgia in some ways, though with almost ten times as many people, it is an entirely different matter in others. Indeed, it is the largest, and far and away the most populous, country under consideration here. As Ambassador Steven Pifer writes in his book *The Eagle and the Trident*, Ukraine's history is deeply interwoven with Russia's. Apart from, perhaps, Belarus, Ukraine may be the former Soviet republic that has the deepest sense of common identity with the Russian Federation—yet at the same time a strong and growing sense of separate nationhood and sovereignty, whether Russians like Putin recognize it or not.

Ukraine and Russia were essentially part of the same ancient polity, Kyivan Rus', from 882 to 1240. Of course, given the huge expanses of central Eurasia, the myriad ethnic and religious groups, the ebbs and flows of invaders, and many other factors, it would be misleading to think of Kyivan Rus' as the equivalent of a strong nation-state with a type of governance resembling the modern era. These were, after all, the Middle Ages, when much of Western Europe was only gradually witnessing the development of the nation-state itself.

Ukraine then experienced several centuries of separate existence. During that long period, various parts of its territory shifted hands on numerous occasions. Lithuanians, Austro-Hungarians, Crimeans, Poles, Russians, even Ottomans exercised some degree of control at times. Then, in 1654, its leaders (of the Cossack group or people) agreed to join Russia, and the accession held until the Bolshevik Revolution. From 1918 to 1921, Ukraine was briefly independent before joining the Soviet Union.[21]

The Soviet decades included enormous pain and suffering. Stalin's rule led to the Great Famine and the death of millions of citizens. Ukraine was obliterated by World War II, losing an estimated 15 percent of its population in the course of the conflict.[22]

Premier Khrushchev famously gave Crimea to Ukraine in 1954. This could be interpreted as an act of great generosity or, alternatively, as little more than an administrative rearrangement given that the constituent republics of the Soviet Union were entirely subservient to Moscow. The fact that the Black Sea Fleet was based in Sevastopol on the Crimean peninsula underscored the degree to which Moscow would hardly have seen this change as reducing its own control of all matters Ukrainian.

Pifer argues that in the years since the dissolution of the Warsaw Pact and the Soviet Union, American policy toward Ukraine has been decidedly mixed in its effectiveness. He asserts that Washington found a good balance of incentives and disincentives in dealing with Ukraine's foreign and security policies. Notably, Kiev was persuaded to denuclearize after inheriting a substantial fraction of the Soviet Union's nuclear infrastructure and arsenal. This decision was accompanied by the 1994 Budapest Memorandum, by which Russia, the United States, and the United Kingdom promised to uphold Ukraine's security—a promise that clearly has not been kept, most notably not by Russia.

If Washington was happy with Ukraine's decision to denuclearize, it was less successful over the years in encouraging domestic and economic reform. Some reforms have been enacted in areas such as the pricing of energy, the transparency of the financial holdings of government officials, and the country's fiscal situation.[23] However, the current Ukrainian state remains mired in corruption and poor management and a fractious political system.[24] The so-called Orange Revolution of 2004–05, as well as the Maydan Revolution of 2013–14, failed to lead to major improvements. If one compares Ukraine and Poland—two former parts of the Warsaw Pact, countries of roughly comparable population and GDP per capita at Cold War's end—it is striking that Poland is now three times richer per person. This divergence in economic fortunes occurred despite the facts that Ukraine has some of the world's best farmland and that it inherited a substantial fraction of the former Soviet Union's high-technology industrial base (though as economist Clifford Gaddy has convincingly argued, the latter was a very mixed blessing for building a post-Soviet economy).[25]

Again, it is important to note that the sense of Ukrainian identity among Ukrainians is quite strong despite the many centuries in which Russia and Ukraine were part of the same country or empire. This and other factors led to strong support for independence when a referendum was held in late 1991, with 90 percent supporting self-determination. These nationalistic sentiments have probably strengthened further since the Russian aggressions that began in 2014. However, while impressing themselves and the world with their strong sense of nationalism, Ukrainians often have found in the last quarter century that their geopolitical value for the West is less than they might have hoped.[26]

Ukrainian identity and nationalism have historically been strongest in the country's western regions. In eastern Ukraine, a higher proportion of the population is ethnic Russian (that is where most of the nation's Russians, who make up 17 percent of the population, live). However, more recently the political line between east and west Ukraine has begun to blur. Political parties based in the east have started to enjoy some support in the west of the country, and vice versa. Anti-Russian sentiment has hardened, as the Donbas war has by now taken 10,000 lives—even if there is still an element of pragmatism in trying not to alienate Moscow entirely among the country's key political parties and leaders.[27] Polls in April 2014 revealed that a large portion of the population in eastern areas, including even the conflict-afflicted Donbas regions of Donetsk and Luhansk, wanted to remain in Ukraine,[28] yet only a modest plurality of Ukrainians overall supported NATO membership as of June 2016, by a margin of thirty-nine to thirty-two (with support much stronger in the west and center than the east or south).[29]

In terms of national security policy, Kiev has sought to strengthen its military with modest NATO and EU help to defeat Russian-aided separatists in the east. It has also maintained support for the so-called Minsk and Minsk II processes (based on pacts negotiated in 2014 and early 2015). These would lift Western sanctions on Russia and accord Donetsk and Luhansk more autonomy in exchange for a cessation of hostilities and standing down of armed units there. However, Kiev has believed that the separatists, and Moscow, should make efforts on the latter matters before it carries out any major initiatives or constitutional changes in regard to the autonomy question.[30] Russia and the separatists have not obliged; thus, the situation remains stuck, and the conflict saw an uptick in violence in early 2017 yet again.

A brief word is in order about Belarus and Moldova. They are the much smaller neighbors of Ukraine. Belarus is essentially just south of the Baltic states, and to the north of Ukraine—thus, like Ukraine, situated squarely between Poland and Russia. Moldova does not share a border with Russia but has a modest-sized Russian-speaking population that has effectively broken off from the rest of the tiny country. It is a very poor and landlocked state, bordering Romania, as well. Like Ukraine, both Belarus and Moldova have historically been at the junction of competing nationalities and cultures and religions, given their locations in central and eastern Europe. Both are dominated by distinct ethnic groups from which their countries draw their names, and their minority populations are not unimportant in size or political weight (roughly 75 percent of Moldova's population is Moldovan, almost 85 percent of Belarus's is Belarussian, with Russians about 6 percent of the former's population and 8 percent of the latter's).[31]

Neither country has had a successful post-Soviet experience. Belarus has effectively been taken over by the autocratic Alexander Lukashenko, a close ally of Russia (even before Putin's rise to power) and strong critic of NATO. He has ruled since 1994, having recently "won" a fifth presidential term in sham elections, controlling the state with an iron fist and little tolerance for dissent or opposition. The country had been reasonably prosperous in earlier times, by Soviet standards, at least. Since the demise of the Soviet Union, it was granted favorable terms for importing energy by Moscow but remained saddled with an obsolete and state-controlled industry.[32] It has not flourished.

Moldova is a very small and weak state. The year 2014 seemed to augur a brighter future, as it featured completion of an Association Agreement with the European Union and also an accord on visa-free travel in Europe,[33] but the country has since experienced numerous changes of government, as well as a huge and costly banking scandal. Its political class is mostly ineffectual; its citizenry is struggling, not particularly organized politically, and not very confident in the nation's effort to build a new democracy out of the vestiges of the Soviet Union.[34] By about a two to one plurality since 2015, its citizens consistently oppose the idea of Moldova joining NATO.[35]

At present neither Belarus nor Moldova seems likely to drive the NATO enlargement discussion. That said, a change in political leadership in either country could lead to new dynamics in relations with Russia and, thus, the broader NATO debate.

ARMENIA AND AZERBAIJAN

The Armenia and Azerbaijan region of the Caucasus is also relevant to the future of security organization and architecture in Europe. The two countries are closely linked with each other—by a common border, by an ongoing "frozen conflict" over the Nagorno-Karabakh region, by their shared history as former Soviet republics. In one sense, the two small states are far away from it all and not particularly germane to the security concerns of anyone besides each other on a day-to-day basis. On the other hand, their potential for further violence could erupt into open warfare again, at which point Russia and Turkey and others might feel the repercussions of the fighting or become involved in it themselves. Indeed, the situation did erupt into a brief period of focused combat in the spring of 2016, when Azerbaijan tried unsuccessfully to benefit from a recent period of military buildup with what some have described as the largest attack in the area in more than twenty years. That may not be the last word in the matter.[36]

Geographically, Armenia and Azerbaijan both border Georgia. Georgia and Azerbaijan essentially create an east-west swath through the Caucasus region that links the Black Sea to the Caspian Sea, with Russia to the north of that swath of land and Armenia to the south. Landlocked Armenia also borders Turkey, of course, and shares a short border with Iran. Technically, Azerbaijan is also landlocked, since its only littoral is along the inland Caspian Sea. In addition to Armenia, Georgia, Russia, and Iran, Azerbaijan also shares a short common border with Turkey, due to a small, separated piece of territory to the west of the main part of the country.

Armenia benefits from good relations with Moscow and is part of the Eurasian Economic Union, along with Kazakhstan, Russia, and Belarus. It is also part of the Collective Security Treaty Organization, along with Russia, Belarus, Kazakhstan, Kyrgyzstan, and Tajikistan.[37] However, it is in a difficult strategic position, with no access to the sea or "global commons" except via one of the four neighboring countries with which it has complex relations. Much of its energy comes from Russia via pipeline through Georgia. As for Azerbaijan, its best foreign relationships include those with Turkey and several western states.

Both countries are dominated by ethnic groups that give the countries their names and languages. Azerbaijan has more than three times the population of Armenia, but the latter has a global diaspora of some 10 million people (Azerbaijan's diaspora is probably as large, though much of it is in nearby Iran). Armenia's actual population has been shrinking due to economic and political challenges. Azerbaijan certainly has its own share of economic problems, but hydrocarbon revenue stimulates at least some sectors of the economy and some regions of the country. In terms of GDP as well as per capita income, it is well ahead of Armenia today. It sends its oil and gas exports to the world via Georgia and Turkey as well as Russia.[38]

Both countries rank in the world's top ten for the fraction of their respective GDPs devoted to their armed forces, due principally to their conflict with each other.[39]

Politically, Armenia has had stable presidential leadership for nearly a decade under Serzh Sargsian, but after constitutional revision, it is soon to make the transition to a parliamentary system and a new head of state. Azerbaijan is closer to an authoritarian regime. President Ilham Aliyev has been in power since 2003 and elections in the country have not been deemed to be up to international standards.

Armenia has a very long history. It was the first nation to declare itself a Christian political system, in the fourth century, based on a tradition with many similarities to the

Russian Orthodox Church. Given its location and small size, it was frequently at the mercy of nearby powers, including the Ottomans and Persians and Russians. The Ottoman Empire ceded eastern parts of present-day Armenia to Russia in the nineteenth century. Armenians suffered genocide at the hands of Turkish forces in 1915, caught up in the rivalry and violence between Russia and Turkey. Like many of the other countries at issue in this book, it made a brief break for independence after World War I and the Bolshevik Revolution, only to be subjugated by the Soviet Union shortly thereafter.

Azerbaijanis are a mix of Turks, Persians, and other groups who settled in areas to the east of Armenia over the course of many centuries.[40] However, the Nagorno-Karabakh region of Azerbaijan is almost entirely populated by Armenians. As such, it was granted special autonomous status in the 1920s by the Soviet Union. That mostly quelled dissent under the coercive Soviet system—though not entirely, as there were protests in the 1960s in which Armenians demanded the territory back.[41] The situation erupted when the Soviet Union broke apart in the early 1990s, leading quickly to a war between Armenia and Azerbaijan that remains ongoing.[42] It is not truly a "frozen" conflict; indeed, it seems possible that having embarked on a military buildup in recent years, and in the absence of any successful international mediation effort (by either the OSCE or Moscow, both of which have tried and failed), Azerbaijan may again escalate hostilities in an attempt to reestablish control of the territory.[43] Meanwhile, the situation remains essentially as before: Armenian forces, aided by Russia, have managed to help the local population establish a greater degree of separation and autonomy than they previously had, but at the price of Nagorno-Karabakh existing now in a sort of political no-man's-land.

Armenia remains in an uncertain place vis-a-vis Turkey, as well. Efforts at rapprochement dating to a 2009 understanding that addressed the history question and other matters have not been translated into an official accord or formal improvement of relations.[44] Armenia has been attempting to strike a balance in ties with Moscow and the West. It is seeking to complement its membership in the Eurasian Economic Union with closer economic ties with the United States and EU, for example.[45]

Armenia and Azerbaijan remain a long way from most of the world's attention, in one sense. But with an ongoing conflict between them, the potential for serious problems that could affect the equities and interests of other parties remains real, as well.

CYPRUS, SERBIA, AND THE BALKANS

Finally, there is the Balkans region, together with Cyprus. This region may be far from Russia geographically, but it is quite important strategically. The Balkans region includes not only Serbia but also Montenegro, Macedonia, and Bosnia-Herzegovina, as well as Kosovo. Macedonia and Bosnia have formal NATO Membership Action Plans; Montenegro has just acceded to the alliance. Kosovo has declared its independence from Serbia, something Washington and more than 100 other countries have recognized, but it remains in a sort of diplomatic and strategic limbo.

All of the Balkan entities at issue are small. Serbia is the big kid on the block with 7 million people (not counting Kosovo), with 85 percent or so of those citizens Serb by ethnicity. Bosnia has just under 4 million inhabitants; Montenegro has about 650,000. Each of those two countries is about 30 percent Serbian. Bosniaks make up half of the population of Bosnia, and about 15 percent of the country is Croat.

Montenegrins make up almost half of the citizens of Montenegro. Kosovo has almost 2 million citizens, more than
90 percent of whom are Kosovar Albanian. Macedonia has
about 2 million citizens, with Albanians the most sizeable
minority.

The Balkans have been a major source of post–Cold
War contention between Moscow and Western governments
going back to the Yeltsin days. NATO's intervention in the
Kosovo war of 1999, an action opposed by Moscow and, thus,
not approved by the UN Security Council, was seen as one of
the original sins of Western and American unilateralism by
many Russians (including Putin, even though he was not yet
president), as discussed in chapter 1. Serbia, with its orthodox
traditions, had been close to Russia for many years. The outbreak of World War I had its catalyst in the Balkans, not least
because of competing Russian and Western interests there.
Yugoslavia formed in that war's aftermath and became a
communist yet partially nonaligned autocracy under Tito
during the Cold War. When Tito died in 1980, the country
managed to hold together another decade, but the end of the
Cold War and the arrival on the scene of Slobodan Milosevic
as the leader of Serbia led to the multinational confederation's
breakup in the early 1990s.[46] NATO intervened to help end
the Bosnian civil war, which was largely a result of Milosevic's
expansionism and sectarian favoritism, in 1995. When it
sought to do something similar within Serbia itself, helping
protect Kosovar Albanians from Milosevic's ravages in 1999,
Russia cried foul.[47]

The twenty-first century has remained complicated for
the Balkans, as well. Serbia began to move politically in a
generally pro-Western direction; Milosevic lost at the polls
in 2000 and was subsequently extradited to the Hague, where

he died in 2006. But Serbs did not feel quickly rewarded for their reforms. The small remaining Yugoslav Federation, made up of Serbia and Montenegro, dissolved in 2006, with the latter electing for independence, and now NATO membership as well.[48]

Kosovo declared independence on February 17, 2008—an action recognized by the United States the next day. More than 100 other countries have done so, as well, as noted, but not Serbia or Russia (or China), and as such, Kosovo is not currently a member state of the United Nations.

With these developments, Serbia has taken several hits. It lost its access to the sea via Montenegro, an important and historic region populated primarily by co-religionists. It also effectively lost Kosovo, also a key part of its history and culture, containing among other things the fabled Field of the Blackbirds, the location of the great 1389 battle that pitted Serbian Christians against invading Ottomans in a struggle that Milosevic exploited when he first came to power.[49] Serbia has become smaller and more isolated in its corner of Europe than when it was a part of a larger federation.

Bitterness over this matter lingers between Moscow and Western capitals. Even in 2016, Russia's RT media outlet (formerly Russia Today) was publishing an article wrongly claiming that Milosevic had somehow been exonerated for his war crimes, not wanting to let go of that earlier issue.[50] Part of the bitterness is, undoubtedly, explained by the fact that these matters are not merely matters of history. In light of existing NATO-related plans for Macedonia, Montenegro, and Bosnia, and the aspirations of many Kosovars not only to fully separate from Serbia but to join NATO, the geostrategic competition between Russia and the West continues in the Balkans. Serbia, meanwhile, is taking gradual steps toward joining the European Union, though it retains some bitterness at the West and some pro-Russian sentiments, as well. At present it does not, therefore, seem interested in NATO membership.

As for Cyprus, the situation is, perhaps, somewhat less fraught, but even in this distant Mediterranean island of just over 1 million, East-West tensions linger. Cyprus was ruled by Britain for centuries until achieving independence in the twentieth century, with a power-sharing formula established for its Greeks and Turks. But a Greece-supported coup in 1974 led to the countervailing intervention of Turkish troops on the northern third of the island, where they remain. Cyprus is now part of the European Union, but the normal terms of association only apply where the internationally recognized government rules, in the southern two-thirds of the island. Both Cyprian governments now express an interest in reunification of some type but acceptable terms have not yet been reached.[51]

Meanwhile, Cyprus remains geographically close to the Middle East and Syria in particular. Its associations with the West could, therefore, have strategic implications in Moscow's eyes if they extended to substantial military cooperation or even NATO membership. Cyprus has also become an important financial haven and vacation getaway for many Russians, constituting one of Russia's few remaining friendly outposts in Europe. While much of the narrative in 2016 and 2017 in the West has been about Russian encroachment on Western democracy, from Moscow's vantage point the broad sweep of history probably looks very different, as Russia has lost most previous close alliances and friendships in eastern Europe and the Balkans over the last quarter century or so. Cyprus represents a partial exception to that overall trend.

CONCLUSION: HOW NATO EUROPE SEES
THE CRISIS TODAY

Although this chapter's main purpose is to understand how the countries that would be at the center of the new security architecture see their interests and their options, it is worth taking stock of some broad sentiments within the existing alliance today, as well. With twenty-nine countries, NATO is a complex entity. Today, several of its longest-standing members are in the midst of major political change of one type or another, several of its newer members are showing signs of internal strain, and all of its nations are sorting through the dual shocks of the refugee crisis combined with the renewed threat of Russian revanchism.

One element of the discussion is what might be termed NATO's front-line states, those bordering Russia or close to it. These countries include Norway in the north, Estonia and Latvia in the northern Baltic region, and Lithuania plus Poland in the southern Baltic/central European area. Of these, the most exposed are the Baltic states and Poland. These are also the places where the United States is carrying out its European Reassurance Initiative, part of NATO's broader Operation Atlantic Resolve.

Taken together, the typical thinking within these four states can probably be summarized this way. First, they are, collectively, rather ardent in their belief in NATO expansion—not only out of gratitude for being included themselves, but out of a belief that an inclusive approach to the alliance's future also stands to benefit close neighbors, such as Ukraine. They would not feel right about denying options to countries like Ukraine that they have benefited from themselves. The original logic of the expansion process saw it as a way to stabilize a whole region, benefiting not just any individual country receiving an Article V guarantee that an attack on one is an attack on all, but its neighbors, as well. At the same time, these four countries are acutely aware of the potential threat posed by Russia in recent times. They do not tend to justify or excuse Russian hostilities of the last few years with reference to the fact of earlier NATO expansion. They do tend to appreciate the sensitivities in the relationships today, recognizing that the current situation has become far more tense and dangerous than when they joined (1999 in the case of Poland, 2004 for the three Baltics).[52]

A word is also in order on Turkey. That nation, on the front lines of the Syrian civil war and among the leaders of the anti-democratic backlash movement in Europe today, has suffered enormously since 2011. Its leader, Recep Tayyip Erdogan, has moved in autocratic directions internally, while encountering a renewal of domestic violence involving Kurdish groups and a huge threat from ISIS and others in the Arab world. Perhaps all that can be said with confidence is that Turkey's new strategic directions are up in the air. Erdogan has changed his thinking considerably already. He has moved toward limited forms of collaboration with Russia and suggested that, perhaps, he no longer insists on regime change in Damascus, after having made the removal of Bashar al-Assad his preeminent goal earlier in the Syrian conflict. Turkey feels simultaneously somewhat abandoned by NATO and in need of NATO, angry at Putin yet unable to afford the luxury of a complete showdown with Russia, and broadly nationalistic yet also at a moment in its history at which most of its key decisions are made by just one man. It is improvising, and where that will lead in the years to come is very difficult to fathom.[53]

As for the rest of the NATO states, a useful crystallization of key attitudes emerges from a poll released in June 2015 that the Pew Research Center conducted over the previous several months. It showed in a nuanced way both NATO's enduring strength as an organization and its members' divided views about just how firmly to push back against Russia. To the extent that these poll results are similar to attitudes today, it suggests that NATO is still serious about holding together as a self-defense organization, but it is not spoiling for a fight with Russia and does not tend to foresee the need for military force.

The Pew study surveyed publics in Poland, Spain, France, Italy, Germany, the United Kingdom, the United States, and Canada. It found that majorities of citizens in a number of key NATO states would not favor the use of force to protect another alliance member in the event of Russian aggression. That would seem, on its face, to ignore Article V of the NATO alliance's founding charter, the Washington Treaty of 1949, which states that an attack on one is an attack on all, and should be treated accordingly.[54] Specifically, Article V says:

> The Parties agree that an armed attack against one or more of them in Europe or North America shall be considered an attack against them all and consequently they agree that, if such an armed attack occurs, each of them, in exercise of the right of individual or collective self-defence recognised by Article 51 of the Charter of the United Nations, will assist the Party or Parties so attacked by taking forthwith, individually and in concert with the other Parties, such action as it deems necessary, including the use of armed force, to restore and maintain the security of the North Atlantic area. . . .

This lack of willingness to commit to an automatic military response may appear to some as tantamount to an invitation to renewed Russian aggression. It seems to raise the scenario of Vladimir Putin again employing his patriotic cyber attackers and "little green men," not just in Crimea but, perhaps, in Latvia or Estonia—former republics in the Soviet Union turned independent nations and, since 2004, members of NATO. Each also has significant populations of Russian speakers that, Putin can purport, want to be reunited with the motherland. Each is too far east for NATO to easily mount a military defense in any case. Operation Atlantic Resolve together with the European Reassurance Initiative only partially addresses the problem. Are such parts of the Western alliance, and perhaps other countries like Poland, therefore, now vulnerable to Russian aggression?

In fact, it would be a mistake to reach this conclusion based on the Pew survey or any other recent polling. While there are, indeed, some troubling findings in the Pew results, on balance what emerges is the picture of an alliance that still provides the West with considerable cohesion, and considerable leverage, in addressing the problem of Putin. Yet Western publics also wisely see the current crisis as one that fundamentally should not have to be solved by military means.

Before trying to chart a path for the future, it is important to summarize not just the headline-dominating findings just noted, but several other key results from Pew, which generally comport with more recent indicators of NATO public sentiment:

- The NATO publics had negative views of Russia and Putin. They seem to have little doubt of who is primarily responsible for the crisis in relations of the last several years, dating to the immediate aftermath of the Sochi Olympics, when protests in Ukraine forced out the country's previous leader, President Yanukovich.

- Publics in five of eight NATO countries surveyed (the UK, France, Spain, Italy, and Germany) opposed sending weapons to Ukraine to defend itself in the current crisis, as did President Obama as a matter of American policy.

- Nonetheless, six of the eight countries had majorities in favor of bringing Ukraine into NATO, with percentages ranging from France's 55 percent to Canada's 65 percent. In Germany and Italy, however, the figures were only about 35 percent.

- NATO countries remained more than willing to employ sanctions against Russia over its behavior. This was true in every alliance member-state that was polled, including Germany, the most pro-Russian NATO state that was included in the polling.

- Although just 38 percent of Germans favored a military response in the event of a hypothetical Russian attack against another NATO member, they remained in favor of sanctions against Russia. Only 29 percent favored a loosening of the current sanctions, unless Russia's behavior were to change.

- Putin remained extremely popular in Russia, with favorability ratings approaching 90 percent; Russians blamed the West, and falling oil prices, for their current economic woes, and not their own government or its policies. (Two years later, in 2017, this basic situation appears unchanged.)

- Forebodingly, most Russians believe that eastern Ukraine, where the current fighting rages, should not remain part of Ukraine but should either become independent or join their country.

Two more key points are important to remember. First, the type of hypothetical Russian attack against a NATO country that formed the premise for the Pew question about Article V was not clearly specified. Perhaps respondents were in some sense wondering if a takedown of several Latvian or Estonian computer networks, or something similar in scale, or a very minor incursion by a small number of Russian forces over a remote border, really needed to be met with NATO tanks. For most Western publics, the advisability of a major military response might well, understandably enough, depend on the nature of the perceived Russian attack as well as the other options available to the alliance.

Second, and related, it is important to remember that Article V does not demand an automatic, unconditional military response by each alliance member. It says, rather, that an attack on one should lead to a response by all—involving whatever means the individual states determine. Specifically, in quoting Article V again, note the phrase that is italicized:

> The Parties agree that an armed attack against one or more of them in Europe or North America shall be considered an attack against them all and consequently they agree that, if such an armed attack occurs, each of them, in exercise of the right of individual or collective self-defence recognised by Article 51 of the Charter of the United Nations, will assist the Party or Parties so attacked by taking forthwith, individually and in concert with the other Parties, *such action as it deems necessary,* including the use of armed force, to restore and maintain the security of the North Atlantic area. . . .

Furthermore, there are two more sentences in Article V, which read: "Any such armed attack and all measures taken as a result thereof shall immediately be reported to the Security Council. Such measures shall be terminated when the Security Council has taken the measures necessary to restore and maintain international peace and security." In other words, the NATO Treaty assumes that a conflict might not be ended by NATO's own response, but only after the UN Security Council has engaged as well.

This ambiguity may risk complicating deterrence, to be sure. It also needs to be reflected upon as a potential indicator of where alliance thinking about possible further enlargement might go in the future. If alliance publics are already skittish about defending the Baltics, it needs to be asked how likely their governments ever will be to invite more members into NATO. Even if they do, it can be questioned whether they would necessarily fight in the defense of faraway friends located right next to Russia. For all of NATO's enthusiasm about bringing in thirteen new members since the Cold War ended, none of these countries was at real risk of Russian attack when they were offered membership. The enlargement imperative was driven much more by the desire to consolidate democracy, stability, and civilian rule in new parts of the continent than by consensus about offering countries protection against a potentially aggressive Moscow.

A more recent set of Pew polls in NATO shows strong support for the alliance today, in all countries surveyed except Greece. In the United States, where Donald Trump spent 2016 denigrating the alliance, a February 2017 Gallup poll showed a whopping support of 80 percent among the American public.[55] But the Pew polling also showed ambivalence in Europe about any increase in military spending. That was before Trump's victory in the United States on November 8, yet was probably still relevant as another indication of most alliance members' longstanding budgetary priorities. Across eleven countries surveyed, positive views about NATO dominated negative ones by a fifty-seven to twenty-seven median margin. Yet most publics had a strong preference for keeping military spending roughly where it was or cutting spending further. (In the typical country, perhaps 30 to 35 percent of respondents favored increasing spending, 45 to 50 percent favored holding the line, and the remainder preferred reductions.)[56]

The overall picture that tends to emerge is one of an alliance where support for current security arrangements is solid, but enthusiasm for new obligations—or even defending new members with force in certain kinds of scenarios and circumstances—is much more limited. Perhaps the enlargement project, however noble its motivations, has now run its full course. That is the question to which chapter 3 now turns.

CHAPTER 3

The Case for a New Security Architecture

Rather than leave the situation in dangerous limbo, it is time that Western nations conceptualize and seek to negotiate a new security architecture for the neutral countries of eastern Europe. The countries in question collectively form a broken-up arc from Europe's far north to its south—Finland and Sweden, Ukraine and Moldova and Belarus, Georgia and Armenia and Azerbaijan, Cyprus, as well as Serbia and other Balkan states.[1] As we have seen in the previous chapter, most though not all are ambivalent themselves about NATO, and where there is interest in joining, it is often due to a recent sense of threat from Russia that could be substantially mitigated by a new security order. Moreover, many existing NATO member states have publics that are already ambivalent about their military commitments to the eastern extremes of the alliance, making the very feasibility and the wisdom of any further expansion dubious. Put differently, NATO could actually be weakened by further expansion, if the core mutual-defense pact that undergirds the alliance were cast into some doubt by a membership that became too large and extended too far. The arrival in power of the Trump administration in the United States provides a golden opportunity to pursue a new vision and a new paradigm. The discussion process should begin within NATO, and then include consultations with the neutral countries themselves. The formal negotiations would then include all the aforementioned states as well as Russia.

Today's situation in Europe, and therefore globally, is highly fraught. At present, no one's intentions are clear. NATO may or may not someday offer formal Membership Action Plans to countries, including Sweden and Finland; it has already vaguely but quite publicly promised to offer MAPs to Ukraine and Georgia. Ukraine is considering a national referendum on the NATO membership concept. It has now suffered some 10,000 fatalities and huge economic decline as a result of Russian-sponsored aggression in its east. Russia may or may not attempt to anticipate and fend off such alliance enlargement with further efforts to annex territory or to stoke "simmering" conflicts as it has from Moldova to northern Georgia to Crimea to eastern Ukraine over the past ten years or so.

Moscow may continue the other kinds of actions and threats it has perpetrated over the last decade, as well. A partial list includes:[2]

- Cyber attacks on Estonia in 2007

- The promulgation of a new foreign policy doctrine claiming the right to defend Russian citizens and business interests abroad in 2008

- Frequent buzzing of the aircraft and ships of NATO countries and neutral states in recent years

- Provocative deployment of Iskander-M nuclear-capable short-range missiles to Kaliningrad

- Large-scale no-notice military exercises near NATO borders that violate the 1990 Vienna Document among OSCE countries

- The abduction of an Estonian military officer in 2014

- An attempt to influence the outcome of the U.S. presidential election in 2016

- Disinformation campaigns involving slander against NATO troops as they deploy to the Baltic states, purporting heinous crimes that, in fact, did not occur

- Apparent deployment of as many as several dozen nuclear-armed SSC-8 ground-launched cruise missiles in violation of the Intermediate-Range Nuclear Forces treaty

The stakes are high. Even war is not out of the question. President Putin or another nationalist Russian leader could elect to take even more aggressive steps. A crisis could be concocted within a Baltic state, for example, that provided a pretext for a limited Russian incursion to "protect" Russian speakers. If conducted quickly and bloodlessly enough, using various methods of deception and so-called hybrid warfare that Russia has been employing of late—including elements such as the non-uniformed "little green men" who became so noteworthy in the 2014 seizure of Crimea—it could quickly create a fait accompli.[3] Perhaps NATO nations would not consider it worth the risk to mount a huge conventional operation, with all the associated risks of nuclear escalation, to liberate a few towns in Latvia or Estonia.[4] Or so Moscow might hope. This prospect might make the operation seem appealing and relatively safe to the Kremlin. Moscow could

decide it was worth the perceived risks if it stymied any further NATO expansion. Indeed, Moscow might even hope
that such a sequence of events could weaken NATO at its
core, by revealing internal disagreement over how to honor
the alliance's Article V mutual-defense pledge in a gray-area
scenario. And once Article V were revealed to be less than
robust in one place, it would inevitably suffer a degree of reduced credibility more generally.

The odds of such a showdown seem low to modest today.
But even a modest risk of a conflict that could in theory
escalate into war among nuclear-armed states is uncomfort-
ably high.[5] The dangers could also grow larger in the future if
relations with Russia continue on their downward spiral.
The acrimony in U.S.-Russian and NATO-Russian relations
also impedes cooperation on other urgent matters, such as
the need for improvements in the security of nuclear mate-
rials worldwide.[6] There is also little reason to think that,
left essentially on geostrategic autopilot, the relationship will
markedly improve in the years ahead. Perhaps President
Donald Trump can change things for the better simply by
turning over a new leaf with Mr. Putin, but both of Trump's
predecessors came to office with the same aspirations and
were stymied. The structural clash of core interests appears
serious and will be difficult to defuse.[7] The investigations over
possibly illicit contact between members of the Trump presidential campaign and Moscow in 2016 have also seriously
dampened the prospects for an easier relationship.

Today, Ukraine and Georgia, in particular, have been
publicly and officially promised future NATO membership,
yet with no specificity about when or how that might be
achieved. As a result, they are strategically exposed. They
enjoy no current benefit of Article V protection guarantees,
yet Russia has extra incentive to keep them in its crosshairs,

since by destabilizing them and raising the prospect or reality of conflict, it reduces to near nil the odds that NATO will, in fact, commit firmly to offer them membership. This half-pregnant state for Ukraine and Georgia is in some ways the worst of all worlds—just enough provocation to Russia to give Moscow reason to destabilize some of these countries, yet no actual protection now or in the foreseeable future from NATO's mutual-defense pact. Except for the Nordic states, these countries are collectively doing badly in economic, political, and security terms, and geostrategic uncertainty about their future is a big part of the cause. As Samuel Charap and Timothy Colton persuasively put it, at present, "everyone loses." That everyone includes Russia, as well.[8]

THE SOVEREIGN RIGHTS OF STATES AND THE PROPER ROLE OF ALLIANCES

A new security architecture for eastern Europe needs to be based on several foundational concepts. The first, as a matter of moral principle and strategic necessity, is that all countries, big or small, east or west, are fully sovereign and have inherent rights to choose their own form of government, political leadership, diplomatic relations, and economic associations. This is as true for Ukraine and Georgia, and other countries of eastern Europe, as for America's traditional core allies or any other nation. They cannot be conceded or condemned to some Russian sphere of influence. A new security architecture must not amount to a "Yalta 2" that, with echoes of the February 1945 summit between Churchill, Stalin, and Roosevelt held in Crimea to discuss the postwar security order, effectively relegates a number of independent and sovereign countries to Russian domination. Indeed, they must be accorded every right to think of themselves as Western. Their future neutrality, or perhaps better described as alliance nonalignment, only concerns formal membership in mutual-defense security organizations; in other ways, they must be able to "align" themselves as they choose.

This principle of complete sovereignty and independence is inherent to the UN Charter. It is also central in the 1975 Helsinki Final Act, with its emphasis on self-determination and territorial security, that was signed by virtually all European countries, including the Soviet Union.[9] Anything short of this standard would invite a return to the great-power politics of the nineteenth and early twentieth centuries, as well as previous eras in human history, which were notable for their frequent interstate conflict and hegemonic wars. Even if it were deemed normatively acceptable that great powers have spheres of influence, there is no natural way to define these that would or could be stable. Once the pursuit of such spheres is condoned, history and logic suggest that great powers will define them in increasingly ambitious and expansive terms, ultimately producing conflict.[10]

It is worth underscoring the point about economics. Without complete economic freedom, a country might sacrifice not only its prosperity but its national security as well. Absent strong economic foundations, a nation will generally lack the ability to build modern and effective security forces. It will also, possibly, squander the self-confidence and strength needed for cohesive governance of its own country and population. To be sure, if there were some specific economic association that sought its own advancement at the expense of others, through mercantilist or other self-serving mechanisms, countries on the outs of any such association could object to its close neighbors joining the group. But the European Union is not of this nature. If countries in Europe not currently part of the EU wish to join it, and the EU wishes to invite them in, Russia has no reasonable basis for objecting.[11] Any new security order must reinforce this essential principle.

Eventual EU membership need not be mutually exclusive with favorable economic relationships that countries such as Ukraine and Georgia might also negotiate with Russia. Indeed, it would be good that they do so, if acceptable terms could be reached.[12]

By contrast, it is more reasonable to discuss whether the security provisions of the European Union—which effectively echo those of NATO—should be extended to any new members. I argue below that they should not be, in fact.

Similarly, the EU's policies on migration are not prejudicial to the interests of Russia, regardless of which countries might join. A Ukraine or Georgia entitled to the free movements of individuals across national borders, as would be implied by EU membership, does not harm Russia. They would not, for example, encourage any brain drain of individuals out of Russia—since the Ukraine-Russia border and associated controls on the flow of people and goods could remain. As such, Moscow should not claim any special right to influence or approve these kinds of arrangements.

In short, and in summary, eastern European neutral states should be in charge of their own political, diplomatic, economic, and demographic destinies. And before approaching Moscow about any discussion on a new security architecture, Washington and other Western capitals should engage in vigorous diplomacy with the nonaligned countries to convey that message clearly and to hear and consider their concerns.

By contrast, security organizations are a different matter, and the option of NATO membership is not one that the

Western nations should presume to be available to any country. There is no inherent prerogative for all countries to join any security organization they wish. Security organizations are not inherent to the Westphalian state system or even the post–World War II UN-supervised international order. They are constructs designed to serve particular purposes for specific countries during certain periods. If well designed, they will improve security first and foremost for their own members, but also for the regional or global order writ large, without prejudice to the security interests of other states. The effort to organize international society is an ongoing one that involves many different layers of interaction and organization among states, with no clear, predominant role for alliances as the ultimate and central feature of that society.[13] Alliances may help in some cases; they may be irrelevant or cause damage in others. No norm of global governance or international order exists that creates an inherent right for additional countries to join NATO; the North Atlantic Treaty Organization charter is not the international equivalent of the American Bill of Rights for its own citizens.

One need not believe in the concept of "offshore balancing" or sympathize with isolationism to believe that Washington should be highly selective in which future alliance commitments, if any, it seeks to take on.[14] Some talk of the importance of sovereign choice for the neutral countries of Europe—but the United States, and other NATO countries, also have their own right to sovereign choice in terms of which countries they pledge to help defend.[15] In 1954, George Kennan emphasized the importance to the United States of the United Kingdom, the western European heartland, Japan, and Russia in world politics, arguing that these centers of economic activity and military potential could not be allowed to fall under the control of a single potential adversary.[16] The United States has devised a grand strategy that places several of these zones, as well as much of the Middle East and several other regions, within its security system. Doubting the value of future NATO enlargement is, thus, hardly tantamount to isolationism—and may be fully consistent with the logic of Kennan's grand strategic thinking.

Indeed, were NATO enlargement to go too far, its integrity and credibility for its core members might be weakened. Promising to risk war to defend faraway lands seen by American citizens as less than central to their own security might lead to a general lessening in the believability of NATO's core mutual-defense pledge—risking deterrence failure as well as the gradual weakening of the alliance from within. There is such a thing as overreach, even for a country with as expansive interests, and as impressive a network of overseas alliances, as the United States of America.

There were a number of ideas promulgated in the aftermath of the Cold War for new European security architectures based on first principles of international relations and the broad lessons of history. It is time to get back to that way of thinking for the currently neutral states of the continent, rather than to somewhat reflexively assume that any and all countries wishing to join NATO somehow should have that opportunity.[17]

Indeed, permanent neutrality is itself a possible element of a security architecture, if chosen carefully and widely accepted by all. Neutrality has not always worked out so well, as with the fates of Belgium and Holland in the world wars. But in other cases, like those of Switzerland and Austria, it has helped ensure the safety and sovereignty of the countries in question while also helping stabilize relations between neighboring powers or blocs.

Some have counseled me not to use the term *neutrality* to describe the status of the eastern European states at issue here under the future security order I propose. They worry that it could be interpreted as a state of complete ambivalence, an unmooring of countries that may wish to be part of the West—a sort of strategic purgatory. However, I have chosen to use the term unapologetically in its strictest sense—neutrality in regard to security pacts with mutual-defense provisions. This sense of the term is well known and, as noted, has numerous historical precedents. Countries remaining nonallied with NATO and, thus, neutral can, according to the security architecture proposed here, remain not only pro-Western but part of the West themselves, if that concept is defined in any other way.

Article X of the North Atlantic Treaty Organization charter states the following: "The Parties may, by unanimous agreement, invite any other European State in a position to further the principles of this Treaty and to contribute to the security of the North Atlantic area to accede to this Treaty." Some could read this to suggest an inherent right of any and all European states to join NATO. That would be a misreading of the treaty—as well as an illogical and unfounded analysis. It is worth underscoring a key operative phrase in Article X: "any other European state in a position to . . . contribute to the security of the North Atlantic area." If NATO membership for another state would not contribute to improving European security, there is no implication or suggestion that membership should be offered. That statement should not be interpreted only to refer to the noble intentions and military burden sharing capacities of prospective new members, but also to their specific geostrategic circumstances. Not all countries that might measure up to NATO standards in political and military terms should necessarily be part of the alliance. It is also worth noting that as NATO expands eastward, its new members get further and further away from the geographic area of the North Atlantic that was intended to be the focal point of the alliance and that gave it its name. Georgia is not even in Europe. We are also now more than a quarter century beyond the Cold War that gave rise to NATO, and its Article X clause, in the first place. The world has changed. Judgment calls about new members are required; not every case is the same, and circumstances are certainly not what they were in 1949.

In this era of Donald Trump—and even in other eras—it is worth putting this argument in more nationalist terms from an American perspective. The United States alone outspends the rest of NATO by more than two to one in its military budget, despite having a GDP that is relatively comparable to the rest of the alliance in aggregate. Another way to say this is that the United States spends more than twice as high a fraction of its GDP on its military as does the typical NATO ally.[18] The United States remains the military backbone of the alliance. Burden sharing is not fair and equal across the alliance. As such, one might observe that European states do not have the inalienable right to expect American military underwriting of their security. Given that the United States is potentially committing the lives of its sons and daughters to the defense of Europe whenever it takes in new alliance members, like other NATO states, it has an inherent right to decide whether such a move makes sense—for its own security, for existing NATO allies, and for Europe writ large.

NATO'S LEGACY AND NATO'S FUTURE

NATO has been a remarkable organization throughout its history. It remains remarkable today. It did much to protect the security of democratic states and to preserve peace in Europe during the Cold War (with very limited exceptions, notably Turkey and Greece's struggle over Cyprus in 1974). It then successfully changed into a mechanism for stabilizing the post–Cold War order thereafter, including in places such as Bosnia and, more recently, even distant Afghanistan. It transformed itself from what was primarily a self-defense organization to an institution seeking to promote democratic governance, civilian control of the military among member states, peace among new member states (some of which had active territorial disputes before joining NATO, as with Hungary and Slovakia or Hungary and Romania, disagreements that NATO has helped hold in check), and broader regional order.[19] It helped several former Warsaw states and the Baltic states solidify their transition to post–communist polities.

Whether post-1989 NATO expansion was on balance a wise strategic move or not, it was well intentioned and nobly undertaken. Even if opposed to it myself throughout the last twenty-plus years, I always saw the argument against expansion as a sixty/forty proposition rather than a slam dunk. NATO did provide real benefits for the new member states, primarily in terms of promoting the quality of their internal governance and civil-military relations, as well as their broader roles in the international order.[20] It may have protected some new members from the kind of Russian meddling that non-NATO states like Ukraine and Georgia have suffered; we cannot know, and thus cannot rule out the possibility. It does not threaten Russia and has taken pains to reduce any plausible bases for any perception to the contrary. Most notably, longstanding members have chosen not to station significant foreign combat forces within the territory of any of the new members admitted since the Cold War ended. Even today, Operation Atlantic Resolve—the effort to shore up NATO's commitment to Poland and the Baltic states by the combined stationing of several thousand troops in those four countries combined—is as notable for its modest scale as its welcome resoluteness. NATO also created mechanisms such as the North Atlantic Cooperation Council and the Partnership for Peace program to reach out in collegial and collaborative ways to Russia and other former members of the Warsaw Pact.[21] The G-7 invited Russia to join its ranks in the late 1990s as well, though Russia later lost that standing when it invaded Ukraine in 2014.[22]

At times, moreover, the whole thing seemed to be working. The first President Bush got along well with President Gorbachev, as did Bill Clinton with Boris Yeltsin. This century, President George W. Bush felt he had a rapport with Vladimir Putin in the early years, and President Barack Obama attempted a "reset" in relations featuring a major change in U.S. missile defense plans for Europe that was designed, in part, to alleviate Russian worries.[23] Russia itself did not always seem so convinced that NATO expansion was a terribly threatening or unfriendly thing.

Yet this is an American point of view. The fact that most Westerners fully believe it does not mean that others can or should be expected to do so. Russians, in general, have not. Whether most truly see NATO as a physical threat, many do see it as an insult—a psychologically and politically imposing antibody that has approached right up to their borders. This attitude is found not only among older former Soviet apparatchiks, and Russia's current hard-liner president, but even among many younger reformers. A striking example can be seen in the eloquent comments of the young Russian scholar Victoria Panova at Brookings in the fall of 2014, for example.[24] Putin in particular seems motivated by a petulant variant of this outlook. But the views may be at least partly sincere. They are also consistent with the way human beings have traditionally viewed the actions of competitor states in the international arena through history.[25] For Americans, history may have ended, at least temporarily, in 1989. For most Russians, it did not. As Richard Betts trenchantly and presciently put it in regard to post–Cold War Russia, "Defeated great powers usually become competitive again as soon as they can."[26]

This train of thought also leads me to some skepticism about the wisdom of the democracy promotion mission associated with NATO enlargement. Yes, it was sincere and noble in its goals, and yes, it did help consolidate democracy as well as civilian control of the military within a number of mid-sized states in Eastern Europe. But it did so at the risk of setting back democracy within Russia itself, by providing a pretext for hyper-nationalists to oppose liberalism and reform. The net effect of these dynamics—more democracy in smaller countries, less within Russia—has not been so clearly favorable to the overall cause of democracy promotion or to the goal of peace and stability in Europe. The literature on democratic peace theory—the notion that democracies do not tend to fight each other—shows that it is not simply about countries holding elections, but that it is those countries that maintain strong and independent institutions and a transparent, fair-minded media that remain peaceful.[27] As such, Russia's early moves toward democracy should not have been assumed to be adequate or irreversible.[28] A NATO enlargement process that set back Russian democracy to help strengthen democracy in much smaller and inherently less powerful countries rested on dubious logic.

All that said, one might reasonably ask how Russia could view a NATO that had no substantial combat formations within hundreds of miles of its borders as a threat. Surely Russians should have seen that Western democracies had become so casualty averse that they were highly unlikely to launch aggressive conflicts abroad. Couldn't Moscow see that, as Bob Kagan famously put it, Europeans themselves were now "from Venus," not interested in fighting any more than absolutely necessary, and much more intent on sustaining their high standards of living than on sustaining strong armed forces? And wasn't the welcome given Russia on the world stage—including in the G-8, establishing a special NATO-Russia relationship based on the so-called Founding Act and from 2002 onward the NATO-Russia Council, forging various nuclear arms control collaborations, tightening economic engagement—further proof of the West's desire to move beyond the Cold War and treat Russia as a true partner?

Even today, the battalion rotations that NATO has committed to conduct in the Baltic states and Poland are very-modest in their military capabilities. They will be respectively led by Britain, Canada, Germany, and the United States (working from north to south, Estonia to Latvia, and then Lithuania, and finally to Poland).[29] They are to be constituted as combat formations, but modest ones, each with about 1,000 total uniformed personnel. Even collectively they stop short of a single robust, integrated, joint-force-capable combat brigade recommended by former Deputy SACEUR General Sir Richard Shirreff and far short of the RAND Corporation's proposal to station the capability for seven such brigades in eastern member states. The NATO-Russia Founding Act of 1997 by which NATO pledged not to carry out "additional permanent stationing of substantial combat forces" is, thus, still being observed—even after Russia's aggressiveness of recent years and even after its violation of the 1994 Budapest

Memorandum under which Washington, London, and Moscow pledged to uphold Ukrainian security.[30]

It is the case, in my view, that some Russians, including President Putin, have whipped themselves up into an unjustified anger over perceived slights by NATO nations. Putin uses that anger to excuse classic bullying and revanchist behavior, which is truly dangerous. Indeed, his regime uses it to provide cover for squelching dissent and silencing opponents at home, including through political violence.[31] Such behavior absolutely must not be appeased.[32] But it is not impossible for a state to be motivated simultaneously by greed as well as a desire for honor and/or a fear of others, as Thucydides timelessly taught us. In other words, some of Putin's sentiments, while not necessarily legitimate or fair-minded, may not fall so far out of the historical norm for human behavior.

It is not only Putin and the older Russian cold warriors who feel put out. Many Russians feel that NATO did not win the Cold War. Rather, a new generation of leaders of their own country had the wisdom to end it. They were then rewarded for their good sense, not only by a reaffirmation of the organization that had been their nation's adversary, but by a major expansion of that very alliance.[33] President Gorbachev had taken a great deal of time to accept the idea of a reunified Germany remaining in NATO. The first President Bush was unapologetic that Germany had the right to do so, but still worked hard with Secretary of State Baker and others to address as many reasonable Russian/Soviet concerns as possible, including a pledge not to station non-German NATO forces on former East German territory.[34] But then, in the ensuing decade and a half, the NATO alliance moved its eastern border 1,000 kilometers east. This is not to say that NATO broke an actual promise never to expand; no such explicit promise was made.[35] However, the discussion over Germany reveals very clearly the Russian sensitivities even about the territory of the former East Germany, to say nothing about countries much closer to Russia.

The perception among Russians that its former adversary was being triumphalist and insulting proved hard to extinguish, especially as Russia endured the hardships and chaos of Yeltsin's Russia of the 1990s. Former Secretary of Defense William Perry pointed out, when opposing immediate NATO enlargement at the end of President Clinton's first term, that Russia would need more time to move beyond the habits and mindsets of the Cold War. Even if some degree of NATO expansion might eventually make sense, he thought that rushing the process could cause severe setbacks.[36] But NATO enlargement occurred anyway—and then did so again in ensuing years. Russian resentments gradually grew. It was not only President Putin, but also former President Medvedev, who opposed this process.[37] Gorbachev criticized the idea of NATO expansion, as well. Other Russian officials, such as former Foreign Minister Andrei Kozyrev, expressed serious reservations as far back as the early to mid-1990s.[38]

In Russian eyes, not just the Kosovo war but also the Western world's reaction to the events of 9/11 challenged any sense that the world's mature democracies were passive, as noted in chapter 1. President Bush's policies of regime change and the freedom agenda seemed that they might even target a state like Russia, even if only by nonmilitary means. The color revolutions in Ukraine, Georgia, and elsewhere made Russian conspiracy theorists think that no region of the world was off limits to the Americans.

Much of this thinking was overwrought, to be sure. But there is little doubt that the United States and other NATO nations were trying to do more than just ensure a peaceful world. They were trying to create a world more in their image, with Western notions of democracy and individual rights at the heart of it—a vision that other countries could find off-putting, especially if they saw it as being promoted in a self-serving way. One can believe in the basic morality and wisdom of the Western approach to governance, but at the same time recognize that it is associated with American hegemony by many other peoples.[39] One can also acknowledge that the United States and allies often make major mistakes in how they pursue that agenda, exacerbating resentments as a result.[40]

NATO's expansion to the Baltic states—not just former members of the Warsaw Pact, but former constituent republics of the Soviet Union—followed by a promise in 2008 to someday invite Georgia and Ukraine into the alliance furthered the sense among Russians that the West's ambitions knew few bounds. As former government official and scholar Angela Stent put it, "[The George W. Bush administration] wanted NATO membership for Ukraine more than Ukraine itself wanted it—even as American officials throughout the post–Cold War period brushed off any willingness to talk seriously to Russia about its own possible long-term membership in the alliance."[41]

In military terms, Russia's anxieties about NATO membership often seemed excessive—but were not entirely without kernels of understandable, even if incorrect, concern. Russia's history and exposed geostrategic position have created a deeply rooted strategic culture that has powerful defensive as well as offensive characteristics.[42] NATO access to bases in new member states could provide the hypothetical capacity for a major military push eastward even if alliance forces are not routinely stationed in such places in peacetime. Moreover, ongoing advances in technologies such as cyber, stealth, and robotics realms could lead to worries that traditional deterrence concepts and conventional military forces might no longer be quite enough to protect core state interests.[43] American attack submarine capabilities may make Russia's ballistic missile submarine fleet less survivable than Russia would like, even today; U.S. strengths in stealth, and in geographic position, give it advantages in air defense against Russia's bomber deterrent as well. Ongoing U.S. research in missile defense may someday produce systems that could pose a meaningful capability against Russia's ICBMs, too (even though today's do not). Russia's declining population and weak economy when contrasted with those of NATO states—currently roughly a $1.5 trillion GDP and less than 150 million people, versus a combined NATO total of $40 trillion in GDP with 900 million people (to say nothing of NATO's fifteen to one advantage in military spending)— may heighten the sense of relative enfeeblement. Russian doctrines like "escalate to de-escalate" that threaten early nuclear weapons employment in the context of a future war with the West sound belligerent and reckless. But they may also reflect a nervousness among Russians that the imbalance of power with NATO combined with advances in weaponry may leave them quite vulnerable in a future conflict, absent such a bold warfighting concept.[44]

So Russia has decided to push back. By the early 2000s, it increasingly had the means to do so, as it emerged from acute economic malaise caused by decades of communism and a turbulent transition to a quasi-market economy.[45] It established some degree of social stability under President Putin, enjoyed stronger commodity prices on global markets, paid off international loans, and regained some of its swagger. And in many Russian minds, the invasions of neighboring sovereign states, and violations of the OSCE and UN charters as well as the Budapest Memorandum that these actions constituted, were justifiable in light of the supposed provocations that had preceded them. That this argument is wrong does not make it purely cynical; many Russians likely believe it quite genuinely.

The importance of Russia's partial economic recovery is easy to miss. Many theories of hegemonic change in world politics might not underline the significance of such a partial comeback of a middle-sized power, since they often focus on the most powerful countries—and Russia, by most measures, was no longer such an entity.[46] But middle powers, especially those with certain great-power attributes and traditions, can push back against others in their own neighborhoods if they choose. That is what Russia proceeded to do, and what it is still doing today. Its economy is not truly healthy; even beyond the immediate issues of sanctions and lower oil prices, President Putin has failed to change an oligarch-based economy that largely benefits him and his cronies. Russian manufacturing is still characterized by what Clifford Gaddy called a "virtual economy," in which many industries actually lose value—they produce goods worth less than their component parts. Corruption remains rife, inefficiency remains pervasive. But Putin did arrest the economic free fall of the Yeltsin years.

Thus, those who believe that "time is on NATO's side" and we only need wait out Putin until his own star dims or Russia's strength further erodes make an unwise argument. How the world's largest country, in possession of nearly 5,000 nuclear warheads, can be outwaited is difficult to see. Already, Russia is far weaker than the West—but even so, it is perfectly capable of making trouble in places where it feels a strong interest and believes it can outmaneuver even much wealthier and healthier nations. Nothing about the trajectory that Russia is now on will change these basic realities over the next couple of decades. Even if it did, living with the kind of danger in Western-Russian relations that we have today is not something the world should blithely do in the meantime, while it is awaiting Russia's supposed future submission.

Not all of the Russian narrative is credible, of course. Many of its arguments are hijacked in favor of a hyper-nationalist agenda that Putin and some of his cronies favor for their own reasons having little to do with the actual merits of the case. If the narrative were so inherently compelling, why would Putin need to prevent serious debate and dissent about it—silencing his political critics and opponents? Russia's behavior has been brutal at times, as well. It has invaded not just one but two former Soviet republics—Georgia in 2008, Ukraine in 2014. It has also refused to withdraw military equipment from Moldova (as required by the Adapted CFE Treaty accord of 1999, with which Russia subsequently "suspended" compliance in 2007).[47] Even having seen Moldova show little interest in NATO membership, Russia keeps its forces there for reasons it claims relate to peacekeeping, but which may, in fact, also preserve its leverage over a smaller neighbor and fellow former Soviet republic.[48]

Thus, no proposal for a new security architecture for central Europe should be made out of a sense of redress in regard to Russia. Although I agree with much of George Kennan's argument when, in early 1997, he called possible NATO expansion "the most fateful error of American policy in the entire post–cold-war era," it is important not to overdo the critique.[49] Russia's reactions were predictable, and predicted. But they have not been justifiable in any objective moral or strategic sense. In practical terms, NATO expansion may have been a misjudgment, and in any event it no longer makes sense in my eyes. But there were reasonable efforts made to assuage Russian concerns, and there were viable arguments in favor of the idea in terms of cementing democracy and peace in Central and Eastern Europe.

Indeed, it is important to make a proposal for a new security architecture with the willingness and ability to walk away, should Moscow begin to engage in negotiations and then escalate its demands—perhaps proposing that some new NATO members be removed from the alliance, or that the alliance itself be somehow recast or neutered. The former idea should be entirely nonnegotiable for the West. The latter could only be countenanced if it preserved NATO's substance while changing some of its procedural modalities or perhaps its name—and that kind of largely cosmetic change would likely not be enough to please Moscow. Thus, there must be clear limitations on how far NATO would bend over backward to please Russia—and there should not be any form of apology from Western capitals as they discuss and negotiate the idea. A proposal for a new security system for the neutral states of Europe should not be a penance for past perceived offenses, given that there were solid reasons for that expansion and that many efforts were made to defuse Russian objections. But at this juncture—with NATO on Russia's doorstep, the enlargement process stalled for reasons that will be hard to overcome, and the level of east-west animosity conjuring up echoes of the Cold War—it should be attempted.

CONCLUSION

NATO has been an excellent organization throughout its history, and even the questionable process of NATO enlargement has been well intentioned. There is no reason the West should feel somehow guilty about the overall preponderance of its power, or believe that somehow a strong NATO is inherently destabilizing. The growth of NATO has, after all, occurred mostly because of its appeal to others. There is also no historical reason to believe that more equal "balances of power" in the world would make it a safer, more stable place.[50] NATO nations should be proud of what their organization has been and what it has accomplished in its long history, and continue to seek to improve its relevance for today's world.[51] But NATO states should rethink the presumption of further expansion and be creative in imagining future security orders for Europe, particularly for those states in the central and eastern parts of the continent that are presently neutral.

There is no guarantee, of course, that President Putin or other key Russian leaders will prove interested in negotiating an East European Security Architecture. They may not want a resolution of the hegemonic competition now underway between Russia and the West in the countries of eastern Europe. Moscow may feel there is no realistic prospect of Ukraine or Georgia in particular being offered membership in NATO, or the EU, anytime soon—weakening the incentive that it might otherwise perceive to create a new and durable security architecture. Putin may be as troubled by the prospect of EU enlargement as NATO enlargement, in which case my proposal would likely do little to assuage his concerns. He may also prefer to keep today's simmering conflicts simmering, with an ultimate goal of further territorial aggrandizement or at least the retention of leverage against smaller countries he sees as within Russia's natural sphere of influence. Putin may further conclude that the sanctions imposed on Russia over the Crimea and Donbas aggressions will weaken or dissipate without any Russian action being necessary, as political forces and leaders change in the West. Putin might well even welcome an ongoing standoff with the West for the additional excuses it provides him for his strongman behavior at home and his pursuit of grandeur abroad.[52] Yet at the same time, if he can claim to be the Russian leader who stabilized the country's economy, rebuilt its military, and halted NATO's further expansion on his watch, he may conclude that the advantages of this kind of deal—along with the lifting of sanctions and greater opportunity for economic interaction with the West that it would include—are in his interest. After all, he has collaborated before with Washington and other western capitals on matters ranging from Iran sanctions to North Korea sanctions to the war in Afghanistan (at least for a stretch). Provided that no accord is proposed without means of verification, and without means of redress in the event of future noncompliance, Putin's possible willingness to do a deal with the West should be explored.

The outcome of any attempt to create a new security architecture is, thus, of course, uncertain. That is all the more reason that Western leaders should pursue it confidently and unapologetically, and not portray it as some compensation to Moscow that Russian leaders might believe to be only an opening bid or an admission of previous wrongdoing. Nonetheless, the negotiation should be attempted. There is little to be lost by trying, provided the West stays true to its principles and consults closely with the neutral states at issue throughout the process. If Russia refuses to negotiate in good faith, or fails to live up to any deal it might initially support (an issue that is revisited in chapter 4), little will be lost, and options for a toughening of future policy against Russia will remain.

CHAPTER 4

Constructing an East European
Security Architecture

It is time to pursue an East European security architecture as a durable means of stabilizing the currently neutral countries of eastern Europe, thereby helping to place the West's relations with Russia on a more solid and predictable foundation.

The mechanisms and security systems that involve Russia and the West today are inadequate to the tasks at hand. Sometimes Russia and the West cooperate on problems, as with the Iranian nuclear challenge and Afghanistan at certain times in the recent past, but sometimes their dealings outside of Europe only intensify animosities, as with the Syrian war to date. Within Europe, the situation is worse, and the available means of addressing the crisis seem demonstrably inadequate to the task at hand. The Organization for Security and Cooperation in Europe (OSCE) has been deeply engaged in Ukraine, but it lacks the political mandate or the operational capacities to address, let alone resolve, core issues. The NATO-Russia Council, set up to create a more equal and effective partnership, has been recently suspended—just when it is needed most.[1] In light of the causes and circumstances of the Ukraine crisis, a bigger idea is needed than simply arming the Ukrainian military, slapping additional sanctions on Russia, or hoping against hope that the current Minsk II diplomatic process will succeed.

The big idea proposed here is this: NATO should not expand further into eastern Europe, along a long arc stretching from Finland and Sweden down to Cyprus and Serbia, including Kosovo. NATO and the United States should work with the neutral states of the region and Russia to develop a permanent alternative security architecture for those countries that would verifiably guarantee their sovereignty and security without NATO membership. It should also ensure complete freedom for their diplomatic and economic activities; they should not somehow be part of the sphere of influence of Russia or any other country or group.

CHIEF ELEMENTS OF THE EAST EUROPEAN SECURITY ARCHITECTURE

A new security architecture for the neutral countries of eastern Europe would be founded on the concept of sustained neutrality for those countries not now in NATO. That is, they would not join NATO in the future. Nor would any of them not currently in the European Union be granted the security guarantees of the EU, should they eventually join that latter body. The only way this could change, assuming full and proper implementation of the new security architecture and continued compliance with it by Moscow, would be if Russia chose not to raise any objections to the idea of expansion in the future—perhaps in a situation where it, too, had elected to seek membership in the North

Atlantic Treaty Organization. Clearly such a day is a long way off.[2]

Ideally, this architecture could be codified in treaty form. The treaty could be simple because the architecture would not create a new organization, though it would formalize certain types of monitoring and verification practices. It would, then, be ratified by key legislative bodies in the relevant countries. In the case of the United States that would, of course, mean the U.S. Senate. Because ratification could prove controversial and could fail, it would be wise to acknowledge the possibility throughout the negotiation process and consider adopting the concept through executive agreement as a fallback alternative. This approach would be less satisfactory, since it would be less binding on future governments in the respective countries. That said, even treaties can be annulled by future presidents (as with the ABM Treaty under President George W. Bush), and even executive agreements can prove durable if in the mutual interests of the respective parties or otherwise difficult to overturn (as with the recent Iran nuclear deal). Moreover, treaties that fail to achieve ratification are often observed for considerable stretches, as with SALT II and the Comprehensive Nuclear Test Ban Treaty.

As noted, the neutral states would also agree not to be covered by the security provisions of the European Union Treaty, even if they did join the EU in its other dimensions. This idea of separating out "security membership" in the EU from economic and political membership was broached by the Dutch prime minister in 2016, though in a less comprehensive and more tactical way than envisioned here.[3] The reason for making this distinction is that, while the European Union is primarily a political and economic entity, it has security dimensions as well.[4] Specifically, under the

2009 Lisbon Treaty, which updated the Treaty on the European Union, EU member states make a commitment of mutual defense and assistance. Article 42.7 states that "if a Member State is the victim of armed aggression on its territory, the other Member States shall have towards it an obligation of aid and assistance by all the means in their power, in accordance with Article 51 [the right to self-defense] of the United Nations Charter."[5] This phrasing is in some ways even more sweeping and unconditional than Article V of the North Atlantic Treaty Organization, which implies that military force would and should be considered in response to an attack on any member state, but does not oblige every other member to an armed action, and invites each to exercise its own judgment. The EU does not require members to forgo formal neutrality or join any alliance. Thus, Austria, Finland, and Sweden are covered by the European Union's security umbrella (and share in its obligations) yet are also still neutral countries. Nonetheless, I believe the EU's territorial security pledges should not be extended to new countries, lest they confuse and complicate the basic logic of the new security architecture proposed here.[6] New EU members could still participate in security-related activities of the EU in areas such as counterterrorism and maritime security, however.[7] They would also be understood to have every right to participate in multilateral security operations on a scale comparable to what has been the case in the past—even those operations that might be led by NATO—provided they were authorized through the United Nations Security Council (where Russia, of course, enjoys veto rights).

The Crimea issue could be finessed separately in various ways. Russia's transgression there could effectively be forgiven, as a show of good faith by the West, and in recognition of the unusual history and character of that Russian-majority region. More realistically, it could simply be put aside, with the United States and other Western nations choosing not to recognize the annexation (and limiting their willingness to participate in certain types of activities or meetings there), but otherwise not treating it as an impediment to relations. Alternatively, some modest number of sanctions could be retained to sustain the objection to Russia's annexation, not necessarily in the expectation that Moscow would someday reverse course but more as a matter of principle. This might be a situation, however, where it could be counterproductive to stand too forcefully on principle, especially if a new security order beckoned and offered the expectation that the Crimea experience would not be repeated elsewhere in Europe.

The Ukrainian civil war would be resolved and Russian presence in the Donbas verifiably reversed under this plan. Minsk II would, in effect, be implemented, and the Donbas region would receive some autonomy within Ukraine as hostilities were ended. Current Ukrainian politics might make the autonomy arrangements difficult to negotiate, but in the context of a broader pact that ended the war, one would hope for flexibility from Kiev.

The "frozen conflicts" in Transnistria in Moldova, as well as South Ossetia and Abkhazia in Georgia, would also have to be resolved as part of this negotiation; so would the status of Kosovo, ideally. In principle, internationally supervised referenda on independence or accession could be conducted in the Transnistria or the autonomous parts of Georgia, provided the mechanisms were transparent and the outcomes verifiable. There would be an understanding that no new "frozen conflicts" would be created on the territories of sovereign states in the future, as well.

By this proposal, Armenia and Belarus could retain their current political and security associations with Russia, notably under the Collective Security Treaty Organization (CSTO), since it seems fair to say that this is not seen as threatening by Western countries. As part of the new security paradigm, Russia should agree, however, not to dramatically expand its own forward military presence in CSTO countries, as a simple matter of reciprocity and fairness.

Under the plan, NATO would not offer new Membership Action Plans to any currently neutral and nonaligned countries. Technically, these MAPs do not constitute a formal plan for eventual membership, and the alliance reserves the right to make an actual invitation at a later date. Practically speaking, they are designed for countries seeking membership, as reflected in the alliance's own official depiction of the program: "The Membership Action Plan (MAP) is a NATO programme of advice, assistance and practical support tailored to the individual needs of countries wishing to join the Alliance." The official language goes on to say: "Participation in the MAP does not prejudge any decision by the Alliance on future membership."[8] But as a practical matter, MAPs have led to membership, and as such, they should no longer be employed.

At present, Bosnia and Herzegovina and the former Yugoslav Republic of Macedonia have MAPs. Under my proposal, MAPS that had not yet resulted in alliance membership by the time of the negotiations would, ideally, be transformed into mechanisms to help usher these Balkan states into a new security architecture rather than NATO itself. Were Kosovo's independence to be fully established at some future point, it, too, would be given the opportunity to be part of the new security architecture, remaining neutral rather than seeking to join NATO.

Preferably, Finland and Sweden would also remain outside of NATO, despite their Western sensibilities and associations.

Historically and practically, they have long traditions of fi-
nessing their security relationships as neutral countries outside of any alliance. The fact that this longstanding aspect of
their strategic cultures is being called into question, especially
in Sweden, at present is a reflection of the acute tensions in
Western relations with Russia. It is hard to believe that NATO
membership reflects the genuinely preferred outcome among
most Swedes or Finns. If forced to choose between East and
West, they will likely choose the latter—indeed, by most defi-
nitions, they are already part of the latter—but more likely,
they would prefer to avoid a stark choice about their future
security associations. As such, a new security architecture that
offered the promise of a much improved and more stable relationship between the Western world and Russia would likely
reduce the newfound openness to the NATO option in these
two proudly self-reliant countries. Should Russia either reject
the idea of a new security architecture outright or fail to uphold its commitments under such a new security system at
some future date, Sweden and Finland, like the other countries considered here, could, of course, reconsider, in consultation with existing NATO states.

While my proposal could, in theory, go forward even if
some or all the existing MAPs with Balkans states went
forward—and, indeed, even if Sweden and Finland joined
NATO, as well—this would not be the preferred course of
action. Especially if the latter sought to join the Western alliance, that decision would implicitly reflect a lack of confidence in the effectiveness of any new security architecture. As
the strongest states among the group considered here, and
the two with arguably the strongest traditions of neutrality,
Finland and Sweden would do much to set the tone for
everyone else's consideration of a new paradigm for the
broader region. Moreover, it is unlikely that Moscow would

trust the intentions of the West, or be favorably inclined to negotiate a new security architecture if NATO expansion was simultaneously proceeding apace, even if in a limited way. Sweden and Finland, certainly, could stay within the European Union, of course, and they could continue to be part of its security pacts and mechanisms, too. Indeed, the mutual defense clause of the European Treaty provides a compromise of sorts for these two Nordic countries, allowing them at least an important symbol of association with the West in security terms without extending all the way to NATO membership.

Most important, as part of the new architecture, NATO's signals to Ukraine and Georgia in 2008 that they would someday be invited into the alliance would have to be walked back. They would be superseded by the new East European Security Architecture (EESA), which would reliably ensure their sovereignty and might prove negotiable far more quickly than NATO membership could ever have been achieved, given current strategic conditions. It is important to underscore that if the new architecture works as I believe it could, and likely will, it will be preferable to NATO membership for the simple reason that it is a far more credible and attainable arrangement, on a much shorter time horizon.[9] Some might argue that Russia's violation of the Budapest Memorandum of 1994, which had guaranteed Ukrainian sovereignty, suggests that Moscow would not uphold its obligations under any new security arrangement. That is possible, and means of verification as well as measures of possible response to Russian transgressions must be developed, as discussed later. It is also worth noting that since 1994 NATO has added thirteen new members, mostly former Warsaw Pact members or former Soviet republics. Doing so did not amount to an explicit violation of any promise ever made to

Moscow, but as has been argued here, it did dramatically change the European security landscape in Russian eyes. By contrast, the new security order would be intended to create a permanent arrangement that covered the whole continent. This would create a much different situation than what followed the Budapest Memorandum.

Of course no one can guarantee it will prove possible to negotiate an East European Security Architecture. Certain neutral states may reject the concept in the hope that NATO would someday reconsider and offer them membership instead. At one level, their acquiescence is not strictly needed, since they are not being asked to take any active steps or join any new organization. On another level it could prove difficult to negotiate this arrangement, designed as it is to enhance their security, over their adamant objections. Their active cooperation would be needed to end the "frozen conflicts"; for example, as noted, Ukraine would need to do its part to implement Minsk II. Ideally, they would take the public step of inviting this new security order after a certain period of consultation.

In fact, there is a good chance the idea will, ultimately, prove appealing to the neutral states, once discussed and explained and refined. Countries like Ukraine and Georgia surely know that, whatever their long-term prospects, there is virtually no chance of near-term NATO membership being offered them, due to their simmering conflicts with Russia and the lack of consensus about further alliance expansion among current NATO members. Yet Russia knows that NATO has had a tendency toward expansion, even when it has gone through lull periods, and bases current policies on that expectation. This current state of affairs is, thus, in many ways the worst of all worlds. An EESA would not create the same perverse incentives or profound uncertainties.

Of course, Russia may very well reject this proposal. President Putin may believe that a state of semi-permanent conflict, or at least severe tension, with the West is in his domestic political interest. He has squelched virtually all domestic opposition and free media, using the notion of a Russia besieged by outsiders to justify his crackdowns.[10] He may also thrive on geostrategic competition with the West, and on the general reassertion of Russian power throughout much of Eastern Europe and the Middle East. Put simply, he may enjoy this latest incarnation of the "great game" more than he lets on. His expectations about Georgia, Ukraine, and other Soviet republics may also extend beyond a desire for their simple strategic neutrality; he may well not rest until they are again within some Russian "sphere of influence" or "zone of privileged interests."[11]

Whether Russia accepted the idea or not, this proposal for a new security architecture will strike some in the West as distasteful or worse. It would allow Vladimir Putin—who has squashed Russian political and civil society and provoked violent conflicts near his own borders—to claim that he was the Russian leader who stopped NATO in its tracks, preventing any further expansion. But we need to keep our eye on the ball. NATO membership for Ukraine and other nearby countries is not a viable means of settling the current crisis in any event; not even the most hawkish voices within NATO are calling for near-term alliance membership for Ukraine or any other central European state. Moreover, NATO expansion was never designed as a way to pressure or punish Russia (except in the eyes of certain Russians, of course), so a decision not to expand is also not a reward. Allowing Putin to claim some degree of vindication is a far less injurious outcome than running an unnecessarily heightened risk of war—and perpetuating a period of poor relations between Russia and the West that impedes cooperative action against other problems of mutual concern in the Middle East and Asia.

Indeed, a negotiated settlement could substantially reduce the risks of direct NATO-Russia conflict—which, while still small, have grown significantly over the last three years. Efforts to assign blame for how we got to this point must not be allowed to stand in the way of addressing problems that could impose enormous costs and risks if left unresolved. For example, a 2015 report by the European Leadership Network details how the intensity and gravity of incidents involving Russian and Western military forces have increased, raising the risk of an accident or military escalation between nuclear superpowers.[12] Such incidents and activities have hardly relented since then. Military-to-military contacts have also been inadequate. They should expand even before a new security order can be constructed, as U.S. Chairman of the Joint Chiefs of Staff General Joseph Dunford has been wisely promoting.[13] But they will almost surely be piecemeal absent a broader strategic understanding between the great powers.

A deal could also substantially improve the prospects that Ukraine can find peace and begin to refocus on political reform and economic recovery. It would also lower the chances of escalation of the current war. Similar considerations would apply to the case of Georgia.

A new security architecture could not be negotiated overnight. In theory the plan is simple enough to be achievable within months, but more likely one to two years might be required to work through various dimensions of the idea. In addition, implementation of a deal once negotiated could take some time—though it should not be a multi-year process.

While negotiations to devise and formalize the new security architecture were ongoing, most aspects of current Western policy should not change. Notably, sanctions should be sustained but, unless Russia escalates its military activities further, they should not be expanded.

Once the EESA was signed, ratified, and at least partially implemented, sanctions on Russia could be lifted.[14] They could be removed step-by-step, in synchronization with the verified withdrawal of Russian forces from the Donbas region of Ukraine and from Abkhazia and South Ossetia in Georgia. Alternatively, once Russia's withdrawal had begun, they could all be quickly lifted as a show of good faith.

Of course if Russia suspended its withdrawal or otherwise violated its commitments, consequences would ensue. Sanctions could and should be reimposed with the same kind of "snapback" automaticity that was worked out through UN channels in regard to Iran's compliance with the 2015 Joint Comprehensive Plan of Action. Similarly, it is difficult to imagine a new security architecture coming into being, or surviving long, if Russia sustained or intensified its covert and nefarious meddling in Western elections.[15] More is said on this later.

RESOLUTENESS AND RESILIENCE

While a new security regime is being negotiated, and even after it is implemented, NATO must, of course, stay resolute in various dimensions of security policy. A new architecture for the neutral states of eastern Europe would likely be stabilizing. But it would not end all problems between Russia and the West anytime soon, so it should not lead to a lowering of NATO's collective guard.[16]

To begin, the United States and NATO allies would not have had to dismantle any existing weapons or bases under an EESA regime. In that sense, the physical steps of creating the new security architecture, and the associated costs and risks, would be quite modest. Nor would NATO denigrate the standing of any existing members, or weaken its commitment to their security, as it attempted to negotiate a new security regime. Even those, like myself, who were NATO expansion skeptics can, and should, acknowledge that its rationale was not crazy—and that it would be dangerous to reconsider the matter. One can argue that it was risky for NATO to expand all the way to the Baltics. But one can also argue that Russia, given the Soviet history of aggressively annexing those countries during World War II, should have been quick to acknowledge that it now owed them every right to determine their future without interference. In any case, what is done is done. There is no undoing Baltic state membership or that of other eastern European states already in NATO. To reopen that debate would risk deterrence failure and war.

Under the proposed EESA, therefore, the United States and other NATO member states should continue to implement their plans to station modest amounts of equipment in the easternmost NATO countries under the European Reassurance Initiative and Operation Atlantic Resolve. This is a modest effort involving some 5,000 military personnel, the main effects of which are not to create substantial forward-deployed combat power but to signal resolve and to create, in effect, a robust tripwire force. It is not objectionable and should continue. Indeed, the four-battalion presence in NATO's east might be expanded modestly, at least until the current crisis in relations can be eased and a new security architecture adopted. The additional U.S. brigade presence now intended as a temporary expedient for 2017 could be

sustained indefinitely, for example. It is at present a complement to NATO's other very modest recent initiatives—notably,
the NATO Response Force (NRF) formed at the 2014 Wales
summit and its newest incarnation as a Very High Readiness
Joint Task Force. Another U.S. Army brigade could be stationed in Germany; the American drawdown there probably
went too far in recent years, anyway.

I do not, however, support those voices arguing for additional U.S. and other NATO brigades, anywhere from two to
six or more in the alliance's east, that some reputable individuals and organizations have proposed. It seems excessive
relative to the likely conventional threat to NATO and, most
of all, more likely to do net harm to U.S.-Russian and NATO-
Russian relations. That action should only be considered if
the Russian threat to the Baltics or Poland substantially in-
tensifies and if the effort to develop a new security architecture for eastern Europe also fails.[17]

Arms sales within NATO can and should continue. Particularly important, and also unthreatening to Moscow, are
systems to improve cyber and command/control resiliency,
to maintain air defense capacities, and to deploy antitank
weapons.[18] Internal NATO dialogues intended to foster
greater defense collaboration and efficiency among key
subgroups of states, such as the Visegrad Group of Poland,
Hungary, the Czech Republic, and Slovakia, should be unapologetically continued, as well. NATO's modest efforts to
increase presence in the Black Sea are worthy of sustain-
ment, too, with an eye toward shoring up the credibility of
commitments to NATO member states bordering that body
of water—Romania, Bulgaria, and Turkey—rather than sig-
naling any intention to bring Ukraine and Georgia into the
alliance.

Capabilities for operating in the Arctic should be modestly expanded, too. Augmentation of U.S. Coast Guard and Navy presence in Arctic waters should not be viewed principally as a matter of rivalry with Russia (or China or anyone else); indeed, climate change and the gradual melting of polar ice, together with changing travel routes, should be seen as the primary impetus. In particular, new conditions argue strongly for an expansion of capabilities such as icebreaking fleets, where the United States has allowed its assets to atrophy.[19]

On missile defense, the Iran nuclear deal may remove the imminent threat of an Iranian nuclear weapon for a decade or more, assuming the deal holds. But the East European Security Architecture is not a near-term tactical adjustment in policy; it is designed as a permanent, or at least long-term, security framework for Europe. As such, Moscow should not be given false impressions that the current relatively relaxed concern in Western capitals about Iran's capabilities will remain relaxed. NATO must keep open its missile-defense options while maximizing collaboration on them with Russia to the extent possible. After the Obama administration did an impressive job of adjusting American missile-defense plans for Europe to create a design that was even less hypothetically capable against Russian nuclear forces than the Bush plan had been, Moscow remained adamantly against it and excoriated NATO for the idea. Rather than kowtow to such pressure, NATO must stand firm in insisting it will protect itself to the extent any future threat may require. To be sure, such systems should be designed to mitigate whatever reasonable Russian objections might be anticipated. They could even be constrained in some way in a future arms control accord. But they should not be precluded by any kind of a deal on a new security system for Europe.

On matters of cybersecurity, information warfare, and asymmetric warfare, NATO must actually step up its game. Russia's behavior in regard to the American elections of 2016 was sufficiently egregious that it cannot be allowed to recur. This means being ready, as in the Cold War, to fight fire with fire. Putin already believes the United States was behind the Rose, Orange, Tulip, and Maydan revolutions. But Washington's efforts in those places were transparent and innocuous, featuring the work of organizations like the International Republican Institute and the National Democratic Institute. Covert and far more calculated efforts akin to what Russia did in the United States, and is attempting in various European countries now as well, should be carried out proportionately if need be. These methods can include not only help for reformist political movements and politicians but also, if necessary, disinformation efforts against the Russian Federation and its top leaders. One hopes that will not be needed.

Then there is the cyber front. Western states need better cybersecurity practices at home. Additionally, there needs to be the development of a set of possible reprisal options should Russian misbehavior continue. The better practices at home have been discussed, for example, in the 2017 Defense Science Board study on cybersecurity and should prioritize, in the first instance, U.S. nuclear forces and central command and control, but extend to key domestic infrastructure, as well.[20] Clearly Russia is not the only potential threat of concern in this regard. As for reprisal capacities, the idea of creating a Cyber Command distinct from the National Security Agency that focuses more on prompt and effective offensive operations makes sense for the United States at this juncture and should not be slowed or stymied because of any attempt to negotiate a new security order.

Responses to the next incident might not be entirely within the cyber realm, given America's relatively greater dependence on cyber infrastructure and, thus, greater vulnerability to an escalating conflict in cyberspace. They could include targeted and proportionate economic responses; for example, prohibitions on the sale of specific American high-tech products to Russia. Cooperation with Russia on space launch, on production of key components of advanced commercial aircraft, and on other advanced technical matters could be curtailed—and once interrupted, a number of these supply-chain arrangements could be very difficult to restore, upping the stakes for Russia. Targeted sanctions against individuals or organizations of the type imposed by President Obama late in 2016 are also useful options.

I need not set out a detailed agenda here. The key point is that nothing about negotiation of a new security pact should blind the West to the potential for other ongoing problems with Russia and the need for measures to protect ourselves against them and also to retaliate—even while attempting to negotiate or preserve a new EESA.

Staying resolute does not, however, mean unnecessarily raising the temperature in Western-Russian relations. As one key domain where restraint is still appropriate, for example, the United States and other NATO countries should not send weapons to Ukraine's military at this juncture. Such shipments may be morally justifiable in some sense, but the most likely consequence would be a Russian counter-reaction, including additional buildup of arms in eastern Ukraine, followed by even more deadly fighting for all sides there, and damaged prospects for successful negotiation and implementation of the proposed EESA. Modest training and provision of some non-lethal arms to Ukraine can continue but should not be expanded while a broader peace deal is pursued—unless, that is, Russia escalates its own involvement in the war.

FUTURE SECURITY COOPERATION WITH
NEUTRAL STATES AND NATO

Another key set of issues concerns ongoing security collaboration of various types that, even today, neutral countries that might be part of a future EESA share with NATO. These activities are legitimate and nonthreatening and, often, important to the security of the participating states. Thus, it will be essential not to interrupt or end them, even with an EESA in place.

Consider first the issue of security assistance. The United States and other Western states already provide limited amounts of security assistance to most of the neutral countries at issue. Much of this support is for helping ensure civilian control of the armed forces and developing means to collaborate with NATO, through the Partnership for Peace program as well as other activities, on security tasks of mutual interest. For example, the Partnership for Peace effort, overseen by the Euro-Atlantic Partnership Council, has recently included twenty-two countries—Armenia, Austria, Azerbaijan, Belarus, Bosnia and Herzegovina, Ireland, Kazakhstan, the Kyrgyz Republic, Malta, the Republic of Moldova, Montenegro, Russia, Serbia, Sweden, Switzerland, Tajikistan, the former Yugoslav Republic of Macedonia, Turkmenistan, Ukraine, and Uzbekistan.[21] Sixteen of these receive some financial support through Warsaw Initiative Funds—all but Austria, Ireland, Malta (with a small exception), Russia, Sweden, and Switzerland.[22]

Take one example of recent activity involving NATO and several Partnership for Peace nations that occurred in

Ukraine in the summer of 2016. Known as Rapid Trident, it was an exercise involving command and field training dimensions, with an emphasis on peacekeeping and stability operations but with potential applicability to other activities, as well. Some 2,000 personnel took part, from a total of fourteen countries—including Ukraine, the United States, Belgium, Bulgaria, Canada, Georgia, Great Britain, Moldova, Lithuania, Norway, Poland, Romania, Sweden, and Turkey. The exercise emphasized key tasks such as countering improvised explosive devices, convoy operations, and patrolling.[23]

Another important example concerns Georgia. That nation has been involved in Partnership for Peace association with NATO since the 1990s. PfP helped provide a framework under which Georgia could send somewhat more than a company-sized unit (typically a couple hundred soldiers) to the peacekeeping operation in Kosovo from 1999 to 2008. Georgia has also been a key contributor to the NATO-led International Security Assistance Force mission, and now the Resolute Support mission, in Afghanistan. It deployed nearly 1,000 soldiers at the peak of the mission in early 2011; at that time, it was the second largest non-NATO troop contributor to the operation, after Australia. It also has a mountain training site, accredited as a Partnership Training and Education Center by the alliance, which offers courses and training to NATO members and other partner countries.[24]

There have also been maritime exercises involving non-NATO countries. Some are tailored to particular purposes, such as cold-weather training involving several allied states plus Finland and Sweden. The Cold Response exercise of March 2016 is one such example. These kinds of activities should also be allowed to continue under a new security architecture—as should maritime exercises emphasizing search and rescue, or environmental surveillance and monitoring, or interdiction of international criminal or terrorist operations.[25] It would make sense to conduct them at a modest scale, however, since large-scale exercises would represent an escalation of security cooperation and could imply an intended focus against Russia.

However, other types of military preparations with the neutral nations motivated by a poor relationship with Russia might be phased out over time. Training on tasks such as antisubmarine warfare, or coordination of contingency planning for possible conflicts against Russia involving the Baltic Sea, should not be continued indefinitely once the relationship with Russia is stabilized—and once the frequent provocations that Russian forces have carried out in recent years have presumably come to an end, a situation that can be monitored and verified.[26] During the negotiation and early implementation phase of the new security order, these activities might be continued but would, presumably, not increase in scale or frequency.

The United States sells very few arms to the group of twenty-two nations that participate in the Partnership for Peace. In 2015, for example, only Sweden, Ukraine, and Uzbekistan received any weapons shipments, for a combined grand total of only about $50 million in value.[27] Similar levels of defense trade should be acceptable in the future, or even modestly more (as the economies of the affected countries begin to grow faster, perhaps).

NATO's Mediterranean initiatives and dialogues, which include a number of Arab and North African states and focus on issues such as refugee flows and Mideastern security, are also important. The threats they address are sufficiently acute that more effective collaboration would be highly desirable.[28] Thus, one would not wish to cap, in any quantitative sense, possible future joint security activities. Most such efforts should involve Russia, too, in some way.

Then there is the matter of Syria. I am not proposing some global "grand bargain" by which all matters over which Moscow and the West quarrel are somehow simultaneously resolved. It is possible, moreover, that the Syrian civil war may be addressed more quickly than an EESA could be created. But it is, nonetheless, worth noting that there is a powerful logic in favor of Washington and Moscow working together in Syria; it is hard to imagine a solution without such cooperation, given the military and political influence Russia now commands there. American and Russian interests in Syria, while in some tension, may not be diametrically opposed.[29] Thus, a new security arrangement for Europe may help grease the skids toward more effective collaboration in Syria (and elsewhere). But, again, I am proposing neither a grand bargain nor linkage, per se.

In summary, ongoing channels of contact and cooperation involving NATO or the EU with the neutral states of eastern Europe should not be precluded under a new security order. But they could be loosely capped in scale and character. The neutral states must not be deprived of the ability to work with the world's best military alliance, or its individual members, on issues of common concern.

What if new circumstances arose? For example, what if the behavior of a country such as China or Iran gave NATO states and the likes of Sweden or Finland or Ukraine or Georgia common reasons for concern? That could, in turn, lead to a desire for larger-scale and more combat-oriented exercises or deployments. A logical corollary of the framework proposed here, however, is that any such activities should be conducted only after close and careful consultation with Moscow—and, ideally, perhaps even with Russian participation.

How does one "loosely cap cooperation" in a way that will not produce inevitable disputes over what types of collaboration are allowable and which are not? It would, admittedly, be difficult, and probably undesirable, to be overly precise about exactly what limits to place on security assistance, arms sales, and exercises. But there is still value in the idea of agreeing that future activities would not generally exceed the scale of past and ongoing efforts in these domains. A useful analogy is the U.S.-China agreement in 1982 that the United States would cap (and gradually reduce) its arms sales to Taiwan.[30] China has argued for years that the agreement, in fact, committed Washington to wind down these arms transfers more quickly than has been the case; the two countries argue over the interpretation of that accord to this day. But the arguments, while sometimes even acrimonious, occur within certain parameters defined by that 1982 agreement that limit the degree to which this issue has infected the broader relationship.

VERIFICATION AND COMPLIANCE

Even if it were successfully negotiated and implemented, a new East European Security Architecture might not be the end of the story, of course. One would need to take the same "distrust but verify" approach to the creation of any new order, as Ronald Reagan famously articulated when negotiating with Soviet leaders.

It is entirely possible that Russia under Putin, or another leader like Putin, is not simply an aggrieved state acting in response to a sense of embitterment and encirclement, but also now fundamentally a revanchist or revisionist power.

(The terms *revanchist* and *revisionist* are often used inter-
changeably, along with the word *irredentist*—and while there
may be subtle differences, all three words imply a desire to
reclaim what was once viewed as a nation's rightful posses-
sions or areas of influence.) In that event, most likely Moscow
would simply not be willing to negotiate the security framework proposed here. But even if it did, it might do so cynically. It might see the architecture as just a temporary truce
and reject it later. Or, it might view it as a means of constrain-
ing the West, and lulling it into a false sense of complacency
while allowing Russia to carry out surreptitious activities in
the states in question. Moscow might also seek to create a climate of intimidation that would produce a ring of partially
subservient states near Russia's borders despite Moscow's
promise to allow full diplomatic and economic freedoms as
endorsed in this proposal.

As such, in addition to sustaining prudent defensive measures like the European Reassurance Initiative and improving preparation against Russian cyber attacks or political
tomfoolery, Washington and other Western capitals need to
devise a rigorous system of verification and a framework for
responding to possible acts of noncompliance or even aggression by Moscow.

The ultimate recourse if the security architecture failed
would be to reopen the possibility of further NATO expansion. Indeed, NATO could indicate to Moscow that, should it
blatantly violate the terms of the EESA, NATO expansion
might actually accelerate in the future—not being constrained
any longer by the expectation that candidate nations would
first resolve their territorial disputes with neighbors before
being considered for membership. But that would be a last and
least desirable resort. More modest steps need to be conceptu-
alized, in advance, as well.

The first challenge is monitoring and verification. A neutral organization like the Organization for Security and Co-operation in Europe would need to have the capacity and the formal responsibility to monitor compliance with the agreement, to handle any future disputes about security challenges faced by any of the eastern European countries covered by the accord and to investigate and adjudicate complaints. With 700 monitors in Ukraine, the OSCE has been key in observing ongoing fighting and tracking the involvement of various parties. This kind of capability, at least on a roving basis, should be sustained under the new EESA. This concept plays to the strengths of an organization like OSCE—which is inherently more about promoting certain norms of behavior and enhancing confidence-building activities than about physically guaranteeing security.

Certain elements of verification could be expected to be relatively straightforward. Monitoring the locations and movements of large amounts of conventional weaponry, as was done for years under the Conventional Armed Forces in Europe treaty (CFE), is not difficult. That treaty involved hundreds of inspections a year at declared sites, with stipulations requiring notification if equipment was moved or repositioned. Aircraft-flying missions through the Open Skies arrangement—which has typically involved some 100 flights per year over various parts of Eurasian and North American territory—can also contribute usefully to the effort.[31] Indeed, in the course of 2014, U.S. intelligence was capable of tracking the movements of Russian equipment so well that, at times, it provided exact counts on the number of heavy military vehicles that had crossed the border with Ukraine. Observers from the OSCE were also capable of careful monitoring of such movements. Journalistic accounts, including interviews with captured fighters, commercially available imagery, and social media are among the available tools that, together, are increasingly likely to notice any clandestine foreign military presence as its scale grows.[32]

Of course addressing the issue of who owns given pieces of equipment can be complex, as demonstrated by the Donbas experience in eastern Ukraine since 2014. So-called Russian volunteers operated in that region, bringing weaponry with them and, at times, transferring it to Ukrainian separatists. Determining who was who required, among other things, sophisticated American signals intelligence—including sources and methods that the United States was not willing to share in all cases.[33] Moreover, Russia retained some degree of deniability for the actions of these so-called volunteers, at least in its own mind, even if most others were not fooled for long. Russia's *Maskirovka* policies can employ a range of tactics— special forces deployed in small numbers and embedded within locally friendly populations, the hiding of military capabilities and supplies within humanitarian supply convoys, and so forth.[34] Fortunately, as the scale and frequency of such activities increase, their deniability tends to decline. In addition to national technical means, and OSCE inspectors, a few other capabilities and methods could be authorized within the EESA, as well. For example, the current observation provisions in the OSCE's Vienna Document should be improved to allow "snap inspections," when countries conduct snap exercises, as suggested by the Netherlands' special envoy for conventional arms control, Lucien Kleinjan.[35]

For modest-scale violations, some form of redress would be needed short of immediate annulment of the entire security architecture. One option, stipulated in the formal document establishing the new European zone of neutrality, might be that in such a situation, other interested parties could temporarily and proportionately offer to step up their own security activities within the same state as desired.

A second option could employ sanctions. Several high-tech sectors where cooperation occurs today could be targeted, for example. Individuals close to Putin could be, too. Greater efforts could be made—perhaps even using NATO infrastructure dollars to leverage public-private investment options—to further harden Europe against the possibility of Russian retaliatory gas export cutoffs. Europe has many more options for its energy supplies now than it used to. Because of its improved pipeline system, as well as options for importing liquefied natural gas, among other possibilities, it is far less vulnerable to Russian embargo than it once was. A concerted Western plan to improve resilience further could be undertaken should Russian behavior become unacceptable again.[36]

If a violation were sufficiently serious, however, and redress could not be achieved, the entire deal could be declared dead. In other words, if, for example, Russia again invaded Ukraine, the United States and other NATO states, as well as the European Union more broadly, would retain the right to respond. Appropriate steps could include reimposing economic sanctions, providing lethal arms to Ukraine's military, or considering NATO membership for Ukraine, even in the absence of a settlement of its disputes with Russia. The United States might, along with other allies, pledge to rapidly establish a military presence in Ukraine with operational units under such circumstances. The terms of the security order should explicitly allow such an option in the event of blatant noncompliance or treaty violation. Washington should not overemphasize these issues in any

negotiations, lest the entire purpose of the effort to negotiate a new security architecture be lost in worst-case discussions that could be interpreted as threats or expressions
of bad faith. But the United States, along with allies, should
make clear that there would likely be significant consequences to any breach of a new security order.

A related issue concerns crises or direct military conflicts.
For example, what if two of the neutral states wound up at war
with each other, or one of them fought a NATO member state,
and Russia used the opportunity to intervene—perhaps purely
cynically, perhaps with some degree of reasonable strategic
logic? For example, if Armenia and Azerbaijan started to fight
again, how might Russia respond—and how should the United
States and NATO react to any possible Russian military activity? In other words, if Russia did not start the fight, and seemed
to have a defensible argument about the wisdom of intervening to help one party or the other, would that be a serious
violation of the new security architecture?

It would be a mistake to think that one could find a single binding answer to this question in advance. Just as the
United States would never forswear any possible interest or
role in a conflict near its own shores, it would be unrealistic
to expect Russia to do so. That said, there would have to be
mechanisms to improve the odds of promptly detecting intervention done under false pretenses. In general, independent investigation of the causes of any conflict would be the
proper response. And, of course, once the immediate issue
was resolved (even if Russia's role were legitimate), Russian
forces would have to withdraw, perhaps in favor of an international peacekeeping force. Moscow could reasonably insist on the same arrangements in regard to possible NATO
intervention in a neutral state of Europe.

CONCLUSION: TOWARD A LONG-TERM VISION
FOR U.S.-RUSSIA RELATIONS

If a new security arrangement were well designed and successfully brought into existence, it could do much to trans-
form NATO-Russian relations. Clearly, it would not be the
only determinant of their future interactions. Events in other
theaters of mutual concern, like the Middle East, would influence politics and policymaking in Russia and the West.
The specific characters and motivations of future leaders in
key countries would have a major impact, as well. Russia's
own ability to build a healthy population and healthy economy would be crucial in shaping the federation's own future
and, thus, the nature of its interactions with the world writ
large. The China factor could be significant in various ways
for everyone, as well, of course.

All that said, there is reason to think that a new security
arrangement for the currently neutral and strategically contested countries of eastern Europe could go far toward de-
fusing hegemonic competition in Europe between NATO
and Russia. It is quite likely the most important single issue
affecting broader U.S.-Russian relations and NATO-Russian
relations in general. Two world wars and the Cold War cen-
tered on the European theater; Europe is the geographic
space that Russia and the West collectively share.

None of this is to say that creation of an EESA would
make everything easy in future NATO-Russia relations.
Russia seems likely to think of itself differently than do most
Western nations for many years into the future. It is doubtful that Moscow will want to join the European Union, for
example (and doubtful that the EU would want Russia any
time soon). Russia's political culture is likely to remain, in

important ways, non-Western and fiercely nationalistic for a long time to come.

Russians are proud of their history and their nation and their state. They also tend to think it is still relevant for ensuring their security. They see a rising China to their east, a highly assertive America and its allies to their west, and trouble to their south. They also have felt embarrassed and anxious over the decline in their nation's cohesion and power after the Cold War. They are not a people who will quickly dismiss the importance of the state; nor do they have many natural partners in building any post–Westphalian system, since they do not feel particular kinship to any other large bloc of nations. Putin may exemplify this attitude most poignantly, but his 90 percent popularity at various points during the Ukraine crisis, the generally favorable reaction of normal Russians to his assertiveness in the Crimea, and the general weakness of civil society and independent media within the country as a whole suggest it will not quickly fade away.

It does not seem realistic to imagine Russia joining NATO in any reasonably short timeframe, either, even after Putin passes from the scene. A Russia within NATO might have been an option soon after the Cold War,[37] but that day is gone and will not easily or quickly return. Most Russians see the alliance as largely anti-Russian in membership, character, and purpose; even after creation of an EESA, such attitudes will not rapidly disappear.[38]

Even if it is incredulous that a future Russia would seek to join NATO, it is not beyond belief that a post–Putin Russian state could look to mend fences and develop a *modus vivendi* with the Western world. Several motivations could drive Russians toward such an outcome. Russia could seek to improve its economic growth and prosperity through more robust trade. It could also see a strong association with the EU or NATO as a useful hedge against Islamist extremism and China's rise. To reach this mindset, Russia would not necessarily have to abandon all security fears, real or imagined, but would have to conclude that the greater dangers came from the south or east (or within) and could be more effectively checked with Western help.

The effect of this kind of policy could be something of a return to the calmer days of NATO-Russian relations of the 1990s—but in the context of a confident and stable Russia. New institutional mechanisms might be created to address matters of common concern; alternatively, existing vehicles such as the OSCE, NATO-Russia Council, restored G8, and UN Security Council might be strengthened. Nuclear arms control might resume, missile defense issues could become less acrimonious, and strategic cooperation on counterterrorism, Iran, North Korea, Afghanistan, Iraq, and Syria could become more standard.

Perhaps more realistic in the foreseeable future, however, is a more modest goal, what Clifford Gaddy and I coined as a "Reaganov Russia." This vision would assume a proud, nationalistic state with a strong military. If the Russian Federation could take pride in reestablishing itself as a successful status-quo power, it might not see the need for revanchism or other aggression.[39] It could pragmatically weigh its own interests across a wide range of policy options, often concluding that it should cooperate with the West on key strategic issues for its own well-being. Freed by greater self-confidence from the kind of anger and embitterment that has characterized recent years, it could cooperate with the West when interests aligned—probably most of the time—and contain the fallout from those situations where interests diverged.

This framework for the future Russian state might envision the defense sector providing technological innovations that could be spun off to help revive the Russian scientific and manufacturing sectors more broadly. Such spinoffs happened often in the United States under Reagan and other Cold War presidents, and in the Soviet Union, too. It is also an idea advanced by people such as defense official Dmitry Rogozin in the modern Russian context.[40]

Of these two categories of possibilities—a generally friendly or pro-Western Russia of some type, and a "Reaganov Russia"—the latter may be the most realistic aspiration we should hold in the West. It may not fit the model of a liberal, genuinely Western Russia that many in the West (and many intellectuals and reformers in Russia itself) might prefer, but a Reaganov Russia could be a more self-confident and self-satisfied and, therefore, less truculent, nation than what we see today.

This outcome could be good news, and a desirable result, for Washington. The West and Russia would appear, in objective terms, to share most global interests on matters ranging from nuclear nonproliferation to counterterrorism to shaping China's rise in benign ways. A Russian strategic perspective that cleared away emotional baggage and allowed a relatively clear-eyed assessment of when and where to cooperate with outside powers should produce a Russia that is easier to deal with. If the highly sensitive issue of NATO can be managed, this could lead to a world in which the Russian state retained a distinctly different character than Western nations, but one with which core interests could be mutually pursued and the threat of direct conflict virtually eliminated. It may be the best we can hope for, and it would be a major improvement over today.

At some point, the Russian polity may change to the point where history, even if not ending, can enter a fundamentally new era. At that point, a new and more inclusive security order might become possible, with Russia as well as many or all of today's neutral states and NATO nations allied in true partnership, whether under the auspices of something still called the North Atlantic Treaty Organization or something else. But that day is clearly far off, and until it arrives the world will be safer and more stable with a neutral zone in eastern Europe.

Notes

CHAPTER ONE

1. Gareth Jennings, "NATO Fighter Scrambles on the Rise in Response to Growing Russian Air Activity," *Jane's Defence Weekly,* April 5, 2017, p. 9; and Eric Schmitt, "Two Russian Bombers Fly Near Alaska, and U.S. Scrambles Jets," *New York Times,* April 18, 2017 (https://nyti.ms/2pzXBhp).

2. Daniel Wasserbly, "Russia's Inventory of Non-Strategic Nuclear Weapons Worries EUCOM," *Jane's Defence Weekly,* April 5, 2017, p. 5; and Alexey Arbatov, "Understanding the U.S.-Russia Nuclear Schism," *Survival,* vol. 59, no. 2 (April-May 2017), p. 61.

3. Jacob Pramuk, "Declassified: Read the Intelligence Report on Russia Interfering with U.S. Election," CNBC.com, January 6, 2017 (www.cnbc.com/2017/01/06/intelligence-community-says-putin-ordered-campaign-to-influence-election-denigrate-clinton.htm).

4. Much of this section benefits from Fiona Hill and Clifford Gaddy, *Mr. Putin: Operative in the Kremlin,* rev. ed. (Brookings Institution Press, 2015), pp. 285–311.

5. Ibid.

6. See Körber Stiftung, "Europa—aber wo liegen seine Grenzen?" [Europe—but where do its frontiers lie?], 104th Bergedorfer Gesprächskreis [104th Bergedorf Roundtable], Warsaw, Königsschloss, 1995 (www.koerber-stiftung.de/fileadmin/bg/PDFs/bnd_104_de.pdf).

7. President William Jefferson Clinton, *A National Security Strategy of Engagement and Enlargement* (Washington, D.C.: February 1995), p. ii.

8. James M. Goldgeier and Michael McFaul, *Power and Purpose: U.S. Policy toward Russia after the Cold War* (Brookings Institution Press, 2003), pp. 208–10.

9. Ivo H. Daalder and Michael E. O'Hanlon, *Winning Ugly: NATO's War to Save Kosovo* (Brookings Institution Press, 2000).

10. NATO's intervention also shook the Russian public. Polls conducted by VTsIOM, the predecessor polling agency to the Levada Center, showed that the share of Russians polled who had a negative view of the United States rose from barely 20 percent to well over 50 percent in the first half of 1999. Levada Center data as reported in Sberbank Investment Research, *Russia Economic Monthly*, July 2014.

11. See Vladimir Putin, "Obrashcheniye Prezidenta Rossiyskoy Federatsii" [Address by the President of the Russian Federation], March 18, 2014 (news.kremlin.ru/news/20603). An English translation is available (eng.news.kremlin.ru/news/6889).

12. Goldgeier and McFaul, *Power and Purpose*, p. 249. For an American diplomat's side of the story, see Strobe Talbott, *The Russia Hand: A Memoir of Presidential Diplomacy* (New York: Random House, 2002), pp. 298–331.

13. Ibid.

14. See Goldgeier and McFaul, *Power and Purpose*, pp. 261–62.

15. Ibid., p. 263.

16. Ibid., p. 264.

17. For a personal account by someone who interacted with Putin during the Kosovo events, see Strobe Talbott, "Vladimir Putin's Role, Yesterday and Today," *Washington Post*, March 21, 2014. Talbott, former deputy secretary of state in the Clinton

administration, described his meeting with Putin in the latter's capacity as head of the Russian Security Council. Putin's role in Russia's intervention in Kosovo, notes Talbott, "remains a mystery."

18. See "Terror Strikes—and Putin Proposes an Antiterrorist Alliance," in Angela E. Stent, *The Limits of Partnership: U.S.-Russian Relations in the Twenty-First Century* (Princeton University Press, 2014), pp. 62–66. Russian military commanders also tried to draw direct comparisons between Chechnya and the NATO bombing campaign in Yugoslavia in a different way, explaining that they were simply emulating NATO's strategy in trying to deal with the terrorist operations in Chechnya. See Michael Gordon, "Imitating NATO: A Script Is Adapted for Chechnya," *New York Times*, November 28, 1999.

19. Stent, *The Limits of Partnership*, pp. 62–63.

20. Ibid., p. 67.

21. Ariel Cohen, *Russia's Counterinsurgency in North Caucasus: Performance and Consequences* (Carlisle, Pa.: Strategic Studies Institute, U.S. Army War College, March 2014), pp. 20–52.

22. Stent, *The Limits of Partnership*, p. 69. This is a quote from an interview that Stent conducted with former Russian foreign minister Igor Ivanov.

23. See the section "Chechnya, Again" in Goldgeier and McFaul, *Power and Purpose*, pp. 267–86.

24. See Vladimir Putin, "Vstrechi s predstavitelyami razlichnikh soobshchestv" [Meetings with representatives of different communities], September 15, 2001 (archive.kremlin.ru/appears /2001/09/15/0003_type63376type63377_28632.shtml).

25. For a detailed discussion of Russian attitudes toward U.S. ballistic missile defense, including extensive interviews with Russian officials, see Bilyana Lilly, *Russian Foreign Policy toward Missile Defense: Actors, Motivations and Influence* (New York: Lexington Books, 2014).

26. The Baltic states secured independence from Russia after World War I. The United States and other countries did not recognize the Soviet Union's reincorporation of the states after World War II.

27. Fiona Hill and Clifford G. Gaddy, *Mr. Putin: Operative in the Kremlin*, rev. ed. (Brookings Institution Press, 2015), p. 304.

28. As an example, see Putin's televised speech to the Russian people given after the tragedy at Beslan. Vladimir Putin, "Obrashcheniye Prezidenta Vladimira Putina" [Message from the President of Russia, Vladimir Putin], September 4, 2004 (http://archive .kremlin.ru/appears/2004/09/04/1752_type63374type82634 _76320.shtml).

29. See Stent, *The Limits of Partnership*, pp. 97–123, for a detailed discussion of Russian responses to the color revolutions and Russian government interpretations of events. See also Condoleezza Rice, *Democracy: Stories from the Long Road to Freedom* (New York: Twelve, 2017), pp. 166–201.

30. For more information on the policies related to the Bush administration's Freedom Agenda, see the George W. Bush archives (georgewbush-whitehouse.archives.gov/infocus/freedom agenda); and Paulette Chu Miniter, "Why George Bush's Freedom Agenda Is Here to Stay," *Foreign Policy*, August 21, 2007 (www .foreignpolicy.com/articles/2007/08/20/why_george_bushs _ldquofreedom_agendardquo_is_here_to_stay_).

31. Stent, *The Limits of Partnership*, p. 10.

32. See, for example, the text of "Cheney's Speech in Lithuania," *New York Times*, May 4, 2006.

33. Vladimir Putin, "Speech and the Following Discussion at the Munich Security Conference on Security Policy," February 10, 2007 (http://archive.kremlin.ru/eng/speeches/2007/02/10/0138_t ype82912type82914type82917type84779_118123.shtml); and Stent, *The Limits of Partnership*, pp. 147–49.

34. Vladimir Putin, "Press Statement and Answers to Journalists' Questions Following a Meeting of the Russia-NATO Council," April 4, 2008 (archive.kremlin.ru/eng/text/speeches/2008 /04/04/1949_type82915_163150.shtml).

35. Cited in Stent, *The Limits of Partnership*, p. 161.

36. Ibid., pp. 238–39.

37. Bobo Lo, "Medvedev and the New European Security Architecture," Centre for European Reform, London, July 2009

(www.cer.org.uk/sites/default/files/publications/attachments/pdf /2011/pbrief_medvedev_july09-741.pdf).

38. Stent, *The Limits of Partnership*, pp. 168–76.

39. Ibid., pp. 211–34.

40. Putin declared Qaddafi's death an "outrage" (*bezobraziye*) in his November 11, 2011, meeting with the Valdai Discussion group, which also covered many of these same issues.

41. "Vladimir Putin's Unshakeable Popularity," *The Economist,* February 4, 2016.

42. Paul Saunder, "Sergey Lavrov: The Interview," *National Interest,* March 29, 2017 (http://nationalinterest.org/feature/sergey -lavrov-the-interview-19940).

43. Vladimir Putin, "A Plea for Caution from Russia: What Vladimir Putin Has to Say to Americans about Syria," *New York Times*, September 11, 2013. (The op-ed was published on September 11 but is listed on the website as September 12.)

44. See Vladimir Putin, "Obrashcheniye Prezidenta Rossiyskoy Federatsii" [Address by the President of the Russian Federation], March 18, 2014, available on the Kremlin's website archive in Russian (news.kremlin.ru/news/20603). An English translation is available (eng.news.kremlin.ru/news/6889).

45. On the cyber dimensions, see Ben Buchanan and Michael Sulmeyer, "Russia and Cyber Operations: Challenges and Opportunities for the Next U.S. Administration," Carnegie Endowment for International Peace, Washington, D.C., December 13, 2016 (http://carnegieendowment.org/2016/12/13/russia-and-cyber -operations-challenges-and-opportunities-for-next-u.s. -administration-pub-66433).

46. Adriana Lins de Albuquerque and Jakob Hedenskog, "Ukraine: A Defense Sector Reform Assessment," FOI Report R-4157-SE, FOI, Stockholm, Sweden, December 2015 (file:///C:/Users/ MOHANLON/Downloads/http—webbrapp.ptn.foi.se-pdf-78b12d4c-19d6-4727-b96b-7faa5ba088dc%20(5).pdf).

47. See, for example, Julianne Smith and Jerry Hendrix, "Assured Resolve: Testing Possible Challenges to Baltic Security," Center for a New American Security, Washington, D.C., 2016, p. 2.

48. In their early analysis of Putin, Herspring and Kipp noted: "Watching Putin deal with Moscow's foreign debt is especially interesting. He wants nothing more than to pay it." Dale R. Herspring and Jacob Kipp, "Understanding the Elusive Mr. Putin," *Problems of Post-Communism,* vol. 48, no. 5 (September/October 2001), p. 15.

49. See Mikhail Barabanov, "Hard Lessons Learned: Russian Military Reform up to the Georgian Conflict," and "Changing the Force and Moving Forward after Georgia," in *Brothers Armed: Military Aspects of the Crisis in Ukraine,* edited by Colby Howard and Ruslan Pukhov (Minneapolis: East View Press, 2014), pp. 74–90, 91–123. France suspended the Mistral contract in late 2014, pending further developments in Ukraine.

50. See Jim Nichol, "Russian Military Reform and Defense Policy," Congressional Research Service, Washington, D.C., August 24, 2011.

51. Christian Le Miere and Jeffrey Mazo, *Arctic Opening: Insecurity and Opportunity* (London: International Institute for Strategic Studies, 2013), p. 84.

52. Tomas Malmlof, Roger Roffey, and Carolina Vendil Pallin, "The Defence Industry," in *Russian Military Capability in a Ten-Year Perspective–2013,* edited by Jakob Hedenskog and Carolina Vendil Pallin (Stockholm, Sweden: FOI, 2013), pp. 128–29.

CHAPTER TWO

1. International Institute for Strategic Studies, *The Military Balance 2016* (Oxfordshire, England: Routledge, 2016), pp. 85–207, 486–90.

2. Bo Ljung, Tomas Malmlof, Karlis Neretnieks, and Michael Winnerstig, eds., *The Security and Defensibility of the Baltic States: A Comprehensive Analysis of a Security Complex in the Making* (Stockholm, Sweden: FOI, 2012) (www.foi.se).

3. Luke Coffey and Daniel Kochis, "The Role of Sweden and Finland in NATO's Defense of the Baltic States," Heritage Foundation, Washington, D.C., April 2016 (www.heritage.org/research /reports/2016/04/the-role-of-sweden-and-finland-in-natos -defense-of-the-baltic-states).

4. Edward Lucas, "Why NATO Needs Finland and Sweden," Center for European Policy Analysis, Washington, D.C., May 2016 (http://cepa.org/Why-NATO-needs-Finland-and-Sweden).

5. See Gordon F. Sander, *The 100-Day Winter War: Finland's Gallant Stand against the Soviet Army* (University Press of Kansas, 2013).

6. Alyson J. K. Bailes, Gunilla Herolf, and Bengt Sundelius, *The Nordic Countries and the European Security and Defense Policy* (Stockholm, Sweden: Stockholm International Peace Research Institute, and Oxford University Press, 2006), pp. 1–11; and Toivo Martikainen, Katri Pynnöniemi, and Sinikukka Saari, *Neighbouring an Unpredictable Russia: Implications for Finland* (Helsinki, Finland: Finnish Institute of International Affairs, October 2016) (www.fiia.fi/en/publication/629/neighbouring_an_unpredictable _russia).

7. Carl Bergovist, "Determined by History: Why Sweden and Finland Will Not Be More Than NATO Partners," *War on the Rocks,* July 13, 2016 (https://warontherocks.com/2016/07/determined-by -history-why-sweden-and-finland-will-not-be-more-than-nato -partners).

8. Russell Goldman, "Russian Violations of Airspace Seen as Unwelcome Test by the West," *New York Times,* October 6, 2015 (www.nytimes.com/2015/10/07/world/europe/russian-violations -of-airspace-seen-as-unwelcome-test-by-the-west.html).

9. For an exception, see Ingemar Dorfer, *The Nordic Nations in the New Western Security Regime* (Washington, D.C.: Woodrow Wilson Center Press, 1997).

10. See, for example, Carl Hvenmark Nilsson, "Sweden's Evolving Relationship with NATO and Its Consequences for the Baltic Sea Region," *Commentary* blog, Center for Strategic and International Studies, Washington, D.C., October 7, 2015 (www.csis.org/analysis/ sweden%E2%80%99s-evolving-relationship-nato-and-its-con- sequences-baltic-sea-region); and Barbara Kunz, "Sweden's NATO Workaround: Swedish Security and Defense Policy against the Backdrop of Russian Revisionism," *Focus Strategique No. 64* (Paris: IFRI, November 2015), pp. 34–37 (www.ifri.org/sites/default/files /atoms/files/fs64kunz_0.pdf).

11. Gabriela Baczynska, "Wary of Russia, Sweden and Finland Sit at NATO Top Table," *Reuters,* July 8, 2016 (www.reuters.com/article/us-nato-summit-nordics-idUSKCN0ZO1EO); and Richard Milne, "Swedes Ponder Joining NATO as Trump Presidency Focuses Minds," *Financial Times,* November 21, 2016 (www.ft.com/content/8b83d6e2-aff9-11e6-a37c-f4a01f1b0fa1).

12. Pauli Jarvenpaa, "Finnish White Paper on Foreign and Security Policy," June 2016 (www.icds.ee/blog/article/finnish-white-paper-on-foreign-and-security-policy); and Prime Minister's Office, "Government Report on Finnish Foreign and Security Policy," *Prime Minister's Office Publications 9/2016* (Helsinki, Finland, June 2016), pp. 23–24 (http://valtioneuvosto.fi/documents/10616/1986338/VNKJ092016+en.pdf/b33c3703-29f4-4cce-a910-b05e32b676b9).

13. Hannah Thoburn, "Border Security in Eastern Europe: Lessons for NATO and Partners," *Policy Brief No. 46,* German Marshall Fund of the United States, January 2017, p. 3 (https://hudson.org/research/13239-border-security-in-eastern-europe-lessons-for-nato-and-partners).

14. See James A. Baker III, *The Politics of Diplomacy: Revolution, War and Peace, 1989–1992* (New York: G. P. Putnam's Sons, 1995), p. 667.

15. See, for example, Angela E. Stent, *The Limits of Partnership: U.S.-Russian Relations in the Twenty-First Century* (Princeton, N.J.: Princeton University Press, 2014), pp. 103–05.

16. Stent, *The Limits of Partnership,* pp. 99–110; and "Bucharest Summit Declaration," Bucharest, Romania, April 3, 2008 (www.nato.int/cps/en/natolive/official_texts_8443.htm).

17. Hillary Rodham Clinton, *Hard Choices* (New York: Simon and Schuster, 2014), p. 239.

18. Center for Insights in Survey Research, "Public Opinion Survey, Residents of Georgia, March-April 2016," International Republican Institute, April 2016 (www.iri.org/sites/default/files/wysiwyg/georgia_2016.pdf).

19. Neil Melvin and Giulia Prelz Oltramonti, "Managing Conflict and Integration in the South Caucasus: A Challenge for the European Union," *SIPRI-CASCADE Policy Brief,* November 2015, p. 4 (www.cascade-caucasus.eu/en_GB/827).

20. See, for example, Maciej Falkowski, "Georgian Drift: The Crisis of Georgia's Way Westwards," Centre for Eastern Studies, Osrodek Studiow Wschodnich, Warsaw, Poland, February 2016 (www.osw.waw.pl/sites/default/files/pw_57_ang_georgian_drift_net.pdf); Giorgi Areshidze, "Georgia's Election Was about More Than Russia," *National Interest,* December 20, 2016 (http://nationalinterest.org/feature/georgias-election-was-about-more-russia-18799?page=2); and Orysia Lutsevych, "How to Finish a Revolution: Civil Society and Democracy in Georgia, Moldova and Ukraine," *Chatham House Briefing Paper,* Chatham House, London, January 2013 (www.chathamhouse.org/publications/papers/view/188407).

21. See Paul Robert Magocsi, *A History of Ukraine* (University of Toronto Press, 1996); and Orest Subtelny, *Ukraine: A History* (University of Toronto Press, 1988).

22. See Timothy Snyder, *Bloodlands: Europe between Hitler and Stalin* (New York: Basic Books, 2010) for an account of the tragic 1930s and 1940s.

23. Fiona Hill and Steven Pifer, "Dealing with a Simmering Ukraine-Russia Conflict," Brookings Institution, Washington, D.C., October 2016 (www.brookings.edu/research/dealing-with-a-simmering-ukraine-russia-conflict).

24. See also, for example, Adrian Karatnycky, "Ukraine: Into and Out of the Abyss," *Politico,* February 17, 2016 (www.politico.eu/article/ukraine-heads-into-the-abyss-petro-poroshenko-arseniy-yatsenyuk); and Wojciech Kononczuk, "Oligarchs after the Maidan: The Old System in a 'New' Ukraine," Centre for Eastern Studies, Osrodek Studiow Wschodnich, Warsaw, Poland, February 16, 2015 (www.osw.waw.pl/sites/default/files/commentary_162_0.pdf).

25. Clifford G. Gaddy, *The Price of the Past: Russia's Struggle with the Legacy of a Militarized Economy* (Brookings Institution Press, 1996); see also International Institute for Strategic Studies, *Strategic Survey 2016: The Annual Review of World Affairs* (Oxfordshire, England: Routledge, 2016), p. 216.

26. Pifer, *The Eagle and the Trident* (Brookings Institution Press, 2017), pp. 1–20.

27. Mikhail Alexseev, "The Tale of the Three Legitimacies: The Shifting Tone and Enduring Substance of Moscow's Ukraine

Policy," *PONARS Eurasia Policy Memo No. 431,* June 2016 (www
.ponarseurasia.org/memo/tale-three-legitimacies-shifting-tone
-and-enduring-substance-moscows-ukraine-policy).

28. See International Crisis Group, "Ukraine: Military Deadlock, Political Crisis," *Briefing No. 85,* Brussels, Belgium, December
2016, pp. 5–7 (www.crisisgroup.org/Europe-central-asia/eastern
-europe/Ukraine/b85-ukraine-military-deadlock-political-crisis);
David J. Kramer, "The Ukraine Invasion: One Year Later," *Journal of
World Affairs,* March/April 2015 (www.worldaffairsjournal.org
/article/ukraine-invasion-one-year-later); and Diane Francis,
"Ukraine's Survivor: Yulia Tymoshenko," *National Post,* October 7,
2016 (http://news.nationalpost.com/full-comment/diane-francis
-ukraines-survivor-yulia-tymoshenko).

29. Center for Insights in Survey Research, "Public Opinion Survey, Residents of Ukraine, May-June 2016," International Republican
Institute, June 2016 (www.iri.org/sites/default/files/wysiwyg/2016
-07-08_ukraine_poll_show_skepticism_glimmer_of_hope.pdf).

30. Fiona Hill and Steven Pifer, "Dealing with a Simmering
Ukraine-Russia Conflict," in *Brookings Big Ideas for America*, edited
by Michael E. O'Hanlon (Brookings Institution Press, 2017),
pp. 349–56; and Daniel Szeligowski, "NATO-Ukraine Cooperation
after the Warsaw Summit," *PISM Bulletin No. 49,* Polish Institute of
International Affairs, Warsaw, Poland, August 4, 2016 (www.pism.pl
/files/?id_plik=22273).

31. Serhii Plokhy, "The 'New Eastern Europe': What to Do with
the Histories of Ukraine, Belarus, and Moldova?" *East European
Politics and Societies* vol. 25, no. 4 (November 2011), pp. 763–69; see
also Central Intelligence Agency, *The World Factbook 2016* (www.
cia.gov/library/publications/the-world-factbook/geos/md.html and
www.cia.gov/library/publications/the-world-factbook/geos/bo
.html).

32. BBC, "Belarus Country Profile," June 24, 2016 (www.bbc
.com/news/world-europe-17941131).

33. See Sonia Liang, "A View from Moldova: Moldova's Rapprochement with NATO," NATO Association of Canada, Toronto,
Canada, May 4, 2016 (http://natoassociation.ca/a-view-from
-moldova).

34. Orysia Lutsevych, "How to Finish a Revolution: Civil Society and Democracy in Georgia, Moldova and Ukraine," *Chatham House Briefing Paper,* Chatham House, London, January 2013 (www.chathamhouse.org/publications/papers/view/188407); International Institute for Strategic Studies, *Strategic Survey 2016: The Annual Review of World Affairs* (Oxfordshire, England: Routledge, 2016), p. 216; and John Lowenhardt, Ronald J. Hill, and Margot Light, "A Wider Europe: The View from Minsk and Chisinau," *International Affairs,* vol. 77, no. 3 (2001), pp. 605–20.

35. Center for Insights in Survey Research, "Public Opinion Survey, Residents of Moldova, September 2016," International Republican Institute, April 2016 (www.iri.org/sites/default/files/wysiwyg/iri_moldova_september_2016_moldova_poll_for_review.pdf).

36. Alexander Clapp, "Prisoner of the Caucasus," *National Interest,* no. 148 (March/April 2017), pp. 43–53.

37. See GlobalSecurity.org, "Collective Security Treaty Organization," March 2014 (www.globalsecurity.org/military/world/int/csto.htm).

38. See BBC, "Armenia Country Profile," June 2, 2016 (www.bbc.com/news/world-europe-17398605); and International Institute for Strategic Studies, *Strategic Survey 2016: The Annual Review of World Affairs* (Oxfordshire, England: Routledge, 2016), pp. 215–16.

39. Central Intelligence Agency, *The World Factbook 2016* (www.cia.gov/library/publications/the-world-factbook).

40. BBC, "Azerbaijan Country Profile," October 16, 2016 (www.bbc.com/news/world-europe-17043424).

41. Yegor Gaidar, *Collapse of an Empire: Lessons for Modern Russia* (Brookings Institution Press, 2007), p. 74.

42. International Crisis Group, "Nagorno-Karabakh: New Opening, or More Peril?" *Report No. 239,* July 4, 2016 (www.crisisgroup.org/europe-central-asia/caucasus/azerbaijan/nagorno-karabakh-new-opening-or-more-peril).

43. Laurence Broers, "The Nagorny Karabakh Conflict: Defaulting to War," Chatham House, London, July 2016, p. 2 (www.chathamhouse.org/publication/nagorny-karabakh-conflict-defaulting-war).

44. John Pike, "Armenia—Relations with Russia," GlobalSecurity.org, 2017 (www.globalsecurity.org/military/world/armenia/foreign-relations-ru.htm).

45. See Melvin and Oltramonti, "Managing Conflict and Integration in the South Caucasus," p. 7.

46. Misha Glenny, *The Fall of Yugoslavia: The Third Balkan War* (New York: Penguin Books, 1992); and Susan L. Woodward, *Balkan Tragedy: Chaos and Dissolution after the Cold War* (Brookings Institution Press, 1995), pp. 21–45.

47. Ivo H. Daalder and Michael E. O'Hanlon, *Winning Ugly: NATO's War to Save Kosovo* (Brookings Institution Press, 2000), p. 176.

48. Euractiv and Agence France-Presse, "NATO and Russia's Influence Dominate Montenegro Vote," Euractiv.com, October 14, 2016 (www.euractiv.com/section/enlargement/news/nato-and-russias-influence-dominate-montenegro-vote).

49. Noel Malcolm, *Kosovo: A Short History* (New York: HarperCollins, 1999), pp. 58–80; and Tim Judah, *Kosovo: War and Revenge* (Yale University Press, 2000), pp. 4–8.

50. Neil Clark, "Milosevic Exonerated, as the NATO War Machine Moves On," *Russia Today,* August 2, 2016 (www.rt.com/op-edge/354362-slobodan-milosevic-exonerated-us-nato).

51. International Crisis Group, "Divided Cyprus: Coming to Terms on an Imperfect Reality," *Europe Report No. 229*, Brussels, Belgium, March 2014 (www.crisisgroup.org/europe-central-asia/western-europemediterranean/cyprus/divided-cyprus-coming-terms-imperfect-reality).

52. See Agnieszka Bienczyk-Missala, "Poland's Foreign and Security Policy: Main Directions," *UNISCI Journal,* no. 40 (January 2016), pp. 101–18 (www.ucm.es/data/cont/media/www/pag-78913/UNISCIDP40-6ABienczyk-Missala1.pdf); Jerzy M. Nowak, "Poland's Security Policy in an Unstable World," *Nacao e Defesa,* no. 125-4 (Spring 2010), pp. 33–48 (https://comum.rcaap.pt/bitstream/10400.26/3071/1/NeD125_JerzyMNowak.pdf); Margarita Seselgyte, "Security Culture of Lithuania," *Lithuanian Policy Review,* 2015, pp. 23–40 (http://lfpr.lt/wp-content/uploads/2015/08/LFPR-24-Seselgyte.pdf); Simon Schofield, interview with Linda

Eicheler, vice president of YEPP, "The Russian Resurgence: A View from Estonia," *Security and Defence,* issue 2, no. 1 (April 2014) (www.hscentre.org/russia-and-eurasia/russian-resurgence-view-estonia); and Luke Coffey, "The Baltic States: Why the United States Must Strengthen Security Cooperation," *Heritage Foundation Backgrounder,* no. 2851 (October 2013) (http://thf_media.s3 .amazonaws.com/2013/pdf/BG2851.pdf).

53. Ali Tuygan and Kemal Kirisci, "U.S.-Turkey Relations under Trump May Hinge More on Turkey Than on Trump," *Order from Chaos* blog, Brookings Institution, Washington, D.C., November 30, 2016 (www.brookings.edu/blog/order-from-chaos/2016/11/30/u-s -turkey-relations-under-trump-may-hinge-more-on-turkey-than -on-trump); and Omer Taspinar, "Foreign Policy after the Failed Coup: The Rise of Turkish Gaullism," *Lobelog Foreign Policy,* September 2, 2016 (https://lobelog.com/foreign-policy-after-the-failed -coup-the-rise-of-turkish-gaullism).

54. Katie Simmons, Bruce Stokes, and Jacob Poushter, "NATO Publics Blame Russia for Ukrainian Crisis, but Reluctant to Provide Military Aid," Pew Charitable Trusts, Washington, D.C., June 10, 2015 (www.pewglobal.org/2015/06/10/nato-publics-blame-russia -for-ukrainian-crisis-but-reluctant-to-provide-military-aid); see also Joshua Shifrinson, "Time to Consolidate NATO?" *Washington Quarterly,* vol. 40, no. 1 (Spring 2017), pp. 109–123.

55. William A. Galston, "How the President Can Reassure Europe," *Wall Street Journal,* February 21, 2017 (www.wsj.com /articles/how-the-president-can-reassure-europe-1487722974).

56. Danielle Cuddington, "Support for NATO Is Widespread Among Member Nations," Pew Research Center, July 6, 2016 (www.pewresearch.org/fact-tank/2016/07/06/support-for-nato-is -widespread-among-member-nations).

CHAPTER THREE

1. Not everyone agrees that disputes over future security architectures are at the heart of the current problems in U.S.-Russia relations, but many do. See, for example, International Institute for Strategic Studies, *Strategic Survey 2016* (Abingdon, England: Routledge, 2016), p. 211.

2. Arianna Rowberry, "The Vienna Document, the Open Skies Treaty, and the Ukraine Crisis," *Up Front* blog, April 10, 2014 (www .brookings.edu/blog/up-front/2014/04/10/the-vienna-document -the-open-skies-treaty-and-the-ukraine-crisis); Ralph S. Clem, "Is This the Right Time to Relieve the Building Pressure in the Baltics?," War on the Rocks, December 20, 2016 (https://warontherocks .com/2016/12/is-this-the-right-time-to-relieve-the-building -pressure-in-the-baltics); Bruce Jones, "Lithuania Sheds Light on 'Information Battlefield' Facing NATO Troops in Baltic," *Jane's Defence Weekly,* March 22, 2017, p. 10; Joanna Hyndle-Hussein, "The Baltic States on the Conflict in Ukraine," *OSW Commentary,* Centre for Eastern Studies, Warsaw, Poland, January 2015 (www.osw.waw .pl/sites/default/files/commentary_158.pdf); Michael R. Gordon, "Russia Deploys Missile, Violating Treaty and Challenging Trump," *New York Times,* February 14, 2017; and Ash Carter, "A Strong and Balanced Approach to Russia," *Survival,* vol. 58, no. 6 (December 2016–January 2017), pp. 52–55.

3. On such concerns, see the Federal Government of Germany, "White Paper 2016 on German Security Policy and the Future of the Bundeswehr," Berlin, 2016, pp. 38, 65 (www.gmfus.org /publications/white-paper-german-security-policy-and-future -bundeswehr).

4. On why even such a discreet conventional operation might entail nuclear risks, see the discussion of "the threat that leaves something to chance" in Thomas C. Schelling, *The Strategy of Conflict* (Harvard University Press, 1960); Scott D. Sagan, *The Limits of Safety: Organizations, Accidents, and Nuclear Weapons* (Princeton University Press, 1993); Barry R. Posen, *Inadvertent Escalation: Conventional War and Nuclear Risks* (Cornell University Press, 1991); and Bruce G. Blair, *Strategic Command and Control: Redefining the Nuclear Threat* (Brookings Institution Press, 1985).

5. On the nuclear dimension, see, for example, Alexey Arbatov, "The Hidden Side of the U.S.-Russian Strategic Confrontation," *Arms Control Today,* vol. 46, no. 7 (September 2016), pp. 20–24.

6. Matthew Bunn, Martin B. Malin, Nickolas Roth, and William H. Tobey, *Preventing Nuclear Terrorism: Continuous Improve-*

ment or Dangerous Decline? (Belfer Center, Harvard Kennedy School, 2016), pp. i–xi.

7. Marta Carlsson and Mike Winnerstig, *Irreconcilable Differences: Analysing the Deteriorating Russian-U.S. Relations* (Stockholm, Sweden: FOI, 2016).

8. Samuel Charap and Timothy J. Colton, *Everyone Loses: The Ukraine Crisis and the Ruinous Contest for Post–Soviet Eurasia* (London: International Institute for Strategic Studies, 2017); on Ukraine and Georgia, see Kimberly Marten, *Reducing Tensions between Russia and NATO* (New York: Council on Foreign Relations, 2017), p. 12.

9. Conference on Security and Cooperation in Europe, "Helsinki Final Act," Helsinki, Finland, August 1975 (www.osce.org /helsinki-final-act?download=true).

10. Robert Kagan, "The Twilight of the Liberal World Order," in *Brookings Big Ideas for America*, edited by Michael E. O'Hanlon (Brookings Institution Press, 2017).

11. There are six countries within the EU that are not in NATO: Finland, Sweden, Austria, Malta, Cyprus, and Ireland. There are, likewise, six countries within NATO and not the EU: Norway, Albania, Iceland, Turkey, the United States, and Canada, plus now Montenegro. Otherwise, each organization has the same twenty-two other members (including, for the moment, the United Kingdom, plus Spain, Portugal, France, the Netherlands, Denmark, Belgium, Luxembourg, Germany, Italy, Poland, the Czech Republic, Slovakia, Hungary, Estonia, Latvia, Lithuania, Romania, Bulgaria, Greece, Croatia, and Slovenia).

12. See Matthew Rojansky, "The Ukraine-Russia Conflict: A Way Forward," in *A New Direction in U.S.-Russia Relations? America's Challenges and Opportunities in Dealing with Russia*, edited by Paul J. Saunders (Washington, D.C.: Center for the National Interest, 2017), p. 31.

13. On this general subject, see, for example, Ernst B. Haas, *Beyond the Nation-State: Functionalism and International Organization* (Stanford University Press, 1964); Hedley Bull, *The Anarchical Society: A Study of Order in World Politics* (Columbia University Press, 1977); and Strobe Talbott, *The*

Great Experiment: The Story of Ancient Empires, Modern States, and the Quest for a Global Nation (New York: Simon and Schuster, 2008).

14. For an argument that seeks to rethink many existing American security obligations, see Barry R. Posen, *Restraint: A New Foundation for U.S. Grand Strategy* (Cornell University Press, 2014).

15. Heather A. Conley and Kathleen H. Hicks, "There Is No Alternative to Sovereign Choice," *Commentary,* Center for Strategic and International Studies, April 27, 2017 (www.csis.org /analysis/there-no-alternative-soverign-choice/?block3).

16. Barton Gellman, *Contending with Kennan: Toward a Philosophy of American Power* (New York: Praeger, 1984), p. 40.

17. See, for example, Richard H. Ullman, *Securing Europe* (Princeton University Press, 1991), pp. 53–82; Ashton B. Carter, William J. Perry, and John D. Steinbruner, *A New Concept of Cooperative Security* (Brookings Institution Press, 1992); and Robert J. Art, "Creating a Disaster: NATO's Open Door Policy," *Political Science Quarterly,* vol. 113, no. 3 (Autumn 1998), pp. 383–403 (www.jstor.org/stable/2658073?seq=1#page_scan_tab_contents). For another recent idea on a future European security architecture, see Simon Saradzhyan, "European Security Reform Holds Key to Breaking Stalemate in Ukraine," *Russia Matters,* Harvard University, October 27, 2016 (www.russiamatters.org/analysis/european -security-reform-holds-key-breaking-stalemate-ukraine).

18. See, for example, Michael E. O'Hanlon, *The $650 Billion Bargain: The Case for Modest Growth in America's Defense Budget* (Brookings Institution Press, 2016), p. 15. See also, Colonel Lars S. Lervik, Norwegian Army, "Deterrence and Engagement," U.S. Army War College Paper, Carlisle, PA, 2017, p. 23.

19. Strobe Talbott, "Why NATO Should Grow," *New York Review of Books,* August 10, 1995 (www.nybooks.com/articles/1995 /08/10/why-nato-should-grow).

20. See Rachel Epstein, "Why NATO Enlargement Was a Good Idea," *Political Violence at a Glance*, University of Denver, Denver, Colorado, September 13, 2016 (https://politicalviolenceataglance .org/2016/09/13/why-nato-enlargement-was-a-good-idea).

21. See, for example, Henry Kissinger, *World Order* (New York: Penguin Press, 2014), pp. 86–95; and Strobe Talbott, *The Russia Hand: A Memoir of Presidential Diplomacy* (New York: Random House, 2002), pp. 92–101.

22. James Kirchick, *The End of Europe: Dictators, Demagogues, and the Coming Dark Age* (University Press, 2017), p. 219.

23. On Bush and Putin, see, for example, Ivo H. Daalder and James M. Lindsay, *America Unbound: The Bush Revolution in Foreign Policy* (Brookings Institution Press, 2003), p. 64.

24. See "U.S.-Russia Relations: Beyond the Crisis in Ukraine," Brookings Institution, Washington, D.C., October 20, 2014 (www .brookings.edu/events/u-s-russia-relations-beyond-the-crisis-in -ukraine).

25. See, for example, Donald Kagan, *On the Origins of War and the Preservation of Peace* (New York: Anchor Books, 1995); and John J. Mearsheimer, *The Tragedy of Great Power Politics* (New York: W. W. Norton and Company, 2001).

26. Richard K. Betts, *American Force: Dangers, Delusions, and Dilemmas in National Security* (Columbia University Press, 2012), p. 194.

27. See, for example, John M. Owen, *Liberal Peace, Liberal War: American Politics and International Security* (Cornell University Press, 1997).

28. Thomas Carothers, *Aiding Democracy Abroad: The Learning Curve* (Washington, D.C.: Carnegie Endowment for International Peace, 1999), p. 15.

29. Jaroslaw Adamowski, "NATO Agrees on E. European Rotational Troops at Warsaw Summit," *Defense News,* July 8, 2016 (www.defensenews.com/story/defense/omr/roadtowarsaw/2016 /07/08/nato-agrees-eastern-european-rotational-battalions -warsaw-summit/86863516).

30. General Sir Richard Shirreff, *War with Russia: An Urgent Warning from Senior Military Command* (New York: Quercus, 2016), pp. xiii–xxix; and North Atlantic Treaty Organization, "Founding Act—on Mutual Relations, Cooperation and Security between NATO and the Russian Federation," Paris, May 27, 1997 (www.nato.int/cps/en/natohq/official_texts_25468.htm).

31. Jackson Diehl, "Risking His Life to Hold Putin Accountable," *Washington Post,* March 20, 2017.

32. See Robert Kagan, "Backing into World War III," ForeignPolicy.com, February 6, 2017 (http://foreignpolicy.com/2017/02 /06/backing-into-world-war-iii-russia-china-trump-obama).

33. For a very good discussion of this perspective, see Raymond L. Garthoff, *A Journey through the Cold War: A Memoir of Containment and Coexistence* (Brookings Institution Press, 2001), p. 377.

34. See James A. Baker III, *The Politics of Diplomacy: Revolution, War and Peace, 1989–1992* (New York: G. P. Putnam's Sons, 1995), pp. 230–59.

35. Steven Pifer, "Did NATO Promise Not to Enlarge? Gorbachev Says No," *Up Front* blog, Brookings Institution, Washington, D.C., November 6, 2014 (www.brookings.edu/blog/up -front/2014/11/06/did-nato-promise-not-to-enlarge-gorbachev -says-no).

36. William J. Perry, *My Journey at the Nuclear Brink* (Stanford University, 2015), pp. 127–29.

37. Fiona Hill and Clifford G. Gaddy, *Mr. Putin: Operative in the Kremlin,* new and expanded ed. (Brookings Institution Press, 2015), p. 308.

38. Pifer, "Did NATO Promise Not to Enlarge?"; and Andrei Kozyrev, "Partnership or Cold Peace?" *Foreign Policy* (Summer 1995), pp. 3–14 (www.jstor.org/stable/1149002).

39. See Robert Kagan, *The World America Made* (New York: Alfred A. Knopf, 2012).

40. A classic discussion of this frequent contradiction between American ideals and American practice is Reinhold Niebuhr, *The Irony of American History* (New York: Charles Scribner's Sons, 1952).

41. Angela E. Stent, *The Limits of Partnership: U.S.-Russian Relations in the Twenty-First Century* (Princeton University Press, 2014), pp. 167–68, 264–65.

42. Stephen R. Covington, "The Culture of Strategic Thought Behind Russia's Modern Approaches to Warfare," *Belfer Center Paper,* Harvard Kennedy School, October 2016; and Eugene

Rumer, "Russia and the Security of Europe," Carnegie Endowment for International Peace, Washington, D.C., June 2016, p. 1 (http://carnegieendowment.org/2016/06/30/russia-and-security -of-europe-pub-63990).

43. Anne Witkowsky, Sherman Garnett, and Jeff MacCausland, "Salvaging the Conventional Armed Forces in Europe Treaty Regime: Options for Washington," Brookings Arms Control Paper Series, Washington, D.C., March 2010, p. 8 (www.brookings.edu/wp -content/uploads/2016/06/03_armed_forces_europe_treaty.pdf).

44. Alexander Velez-Green, "The Unsettling View from Moscow: Russia's Strategic Debate on a Doctrine of Pre-emption," Center for a New American Security, Washington, D.C., April 2017 (https://www .cnas.org/publications/reports/the-unsettling-view-from-moscow).

45. See Clifford G. Gaddy and Barry W. Ickes, *Russia's Virtual Economy* (Brookings Institution Press, 2002); and Fiona Hill and Clifford Gaddy, *The Siberian Curse: How Communist Planners Left Russia Out in the Cold* (Brookings Institution Press, 2003).

46. A classic is Robert Gilpin, *War and Change in World Politics* (Cambridge University Press, 1981).

47. Witkowsky and others, Salvaging the Conventional Armed Forces in Europe Treaty Regime," p. 2.

48. See, for example, "Moldova: No Support for NATO Involvement in Transnistria Dispute," EurasiaNet.org, July 28, 2016 (www .eurasianet.org/node/79901).

49. George F. Kennan, "A Fateful Error," *New York Times,* February 5, 1997 (www.netwargamingitalia.net/forum/resources /george-f-kennan-a-fateful-error.35).

50. Stephen M. Walt, *The Origins of Alliances* (Cornell University Press, 1987); Geoffrey Blainey, *The Causes of War* (New York: Free Press, 1973), pp. 245–49.

51. On this agenda, see, for example, Alexander Mattelaer, "The NATO Warsaw Summit: How to Strengthen Alliance Cohesion," *Strategic Forum No. 296* (Washington, D.C.: Institute for National Strategic Studies, National Defense University, June 2016) (ndupress.ndu.edu); see also Karl-Heinz Kamp, "Why NATO Needs a New Strategic Concept," *NATO Defense College Report* (Rome, Italy: NATO Defense College, 2016).

52. See, for example, David Sattar, "The Character of Russia," *Montreal Review,* January 2012 (www.themontrealreview.com /2009/The-Character-of-Russia-by-David-Satter.php).

CHAPTER FOUR

1. Des Browne, Igor S. Ivanov, and Sam Nunn, "Securing the Euro-Atlantic Community," *Project Syndicate,* February 3, 2015 (www.project-syndicate.org/commentary/ukraine-russia-crisis -european-leadership-by-des- browne-et-al-2015-02).

2. For a related view, see Terry Atlas, "Brzezinski Sees Finlandization of Ukraine as Deal Maker," Bloomberg.com, April 12, 2014 (www.bloomberg.com/news/articles/2014-04-11/brzezinski -sees-finlandization-of-ukraine-as-deal-maker); and Henry A. Kissinger, "To Settle the Ukraine Crisis, Start at the End," *Washington Post,* March 5, 2014.

3. Laurence Norman and Maarten van Tartwijk, "Dutch Premier's Demands Cast New Doubt over EU-Ukraine Pact," *Wall Street Journal,* October 20, 2016.

4. For a good concise history of the European Union, which highlights that security and foreign policy have typically not been the central issues driving its creation or operations, see William I. Hitchcock, *The Struggle for Europe: The Turbulent History of a Divided Continent, 1945–2002* (New York: Doubleday, 2002), pp. 435–64; and Tony Judt, *Postwar: A History of Europe since 1945* (New York: Penguin Press, 2005), pp. 732–36.

5. European Union External Action, "Shaping of a Common Security and Defense Policy," Brussels, Belgium, July 2016 (https:// eeas.europa.eu/topics/nuclear-safety/5388/shaping-of-a-common -security-and-defence-policy-_en). By contrast, Article V of the North Atlantic Treaty Organization reads: "The Parties agree that an armed attack against one or more of them in Europe or North America shall be considered an attack against them all and consequently they agree that, if such an armed attack occurs, each of them, in exercise of the right of individual or collective self-defence recognised by Article 51 of the Charter of the United Nations, will assist the Party or Parties so attacked by taking forthwith, individually and in concert with the other Parties, such

action as it deems necessary, including the use of armed force, to restore and maintain the security of the North Atlantic area." See North Atlantic Treaty Organization, "The North Atlantic Treaty," Washington, D.C., April 4, 1949 (www.nato.int/cps/en/natohq /official_texts_17120.htm).

6. The Vienna-based Organization for Security and Coopera- tion in Europe is yet another organization with a number of important security missions but no standing military capability, a $150 million annual budget, and an inclusive membership. Thus, there should be no issue in sustaining it and including as many European states as wish to participate in its dialogues, oversight activities for certain purposes such as arms control or confidence building, and occasional small field missions with a combined personnel tally today of some 3,000 across seventeen countries. See Nuclear Threat Initiative, "Organization for Security and Co- operation in Europe," Washington, D.C., April 2015 (www.nti.org /learn/treaties-and-regimes/organization-cooperation-and -security-europe-osce); and Organization for Security and Coop- eration in Europe, "What Is the OSCE?" Vienna, Austria, March 2016 (www.osce.org/whatistheosce/factsheet?download=true).

7. Nicole Gnesotto, "Strategie de securite de l'UE: pourquoi et comment renouveler notre approche," *Les Carnets du Caps,* no. 23 (Summer-Autumn 2016), pp. 67–82.

8. North Atlantic Treaty Organization, "Membership Action Plan (MAP)," Brussels, Belgium, December 4, 2015 (www.nato.int /cps/en/natohq/topics_37356.htm).

9. For a related view, see comments of General Sir Richard Shirreff, former deputy supreme allied commander/Europe, at the Brookings Institution, Washington, D.C., October 19, 2016 (www .brookings.edu).

10. Julianne Smith and Adam Twardowski, "The Future of U.S.- Russia Relations," Center for a New American Security, Washing- ton, D.C., January 2017, p. 8 (www.cnas.org/publications/reports /the-future-of-u-s-russia-relations).

11. See, for example, Taras Kuzio, "Why Vladimir Putin Is Angry with the West: Understanding the Drivers of Russia's Information, Cyber and Hybrid War," *Security Policy Working*

Paper No. 7/2017, Federal Academy for Security Policy, Berlin, Germany, February 2017 (www.baks.bund.de/sites/baks010/files /working_paper_2017_07.pdf).

12. Ian Kearns, Lukasz Kulesa, and Thomas Frear, "Preparing for the Worst: Are Russian and NATO Military Exercises Making War in Europe More Likely?," European Leadership Network, London, August 12, 2015 (www.europeanleadershipnetwork.org /preparing-for-the-worst-are-russian-and-nato-military -exercises-making-war-in-europe-more-likely_2997.html).

13. Eugene Rumer, Richard Sokolsky, and Andrew S. Weiss, "Trump and Russia: The Right Way to Manage Relations," *Foreign Affairs,* vol. 96, no. 2 (March/April 2017), p. 16.

14. See Michael O'Hanlon and Jeremy Shapiro, "Crafting a Win-Win-Win for Russia, Ukraine, and the West," *Washington Post,* December 7, 2015 (http://www.brookings.edu/research/opinions/2014 /12/07-russia-ukraine-ohanlon-shapiro).

15. For a compelling argument about the significance of Russian efforts to interfere with Western democracy, see address of Senator Christopher Coons, Brookings Institution, Washington, D.C., April 6, 2017 (www.brookings.edu/blog/brookings-now /2017/04/06/putin-undeclared-war-on-international-order).

16. For an argument about the importance of resoluteness, see Derek Chollet, Eric S. Edelman, Michèle Flournoy, Stephen J. Hadley, Martin S. Indyk, Bruce Jones, Robert Kagan, Kristen Silverberg, Jake Sullivan, and Thomas Wright, "Building Situations of Strength: A National Security Strategy for the United States" (Washington, D.C.: Brookings, 2017) (www.brookings.edu/research/building -situations-of-strength).

17. See, for example, Philip M. Breedlove, "NATO's Next Act: How to Handle Russia and Other Threats," *Foreign Affairs,* vol. 95, no. 4 (July/August 2016), p. 104.

18. See Robert Beckhusen, "The Only Way to Beat Russia in a War over the Baltics," *National Interest* blog, February 6, 2017 (http://nationalinterest.org/blog/the-buzz/the-only-way-beat -russia-war-over-the-baltics-19336).

19. See "A Conversation with Commandant of the U.S. Coast Guard Admiral Paul F. Zukunft," Brookings Institution, Washing-

ton, D.C., November 29, 2016 (www.brookings.edu/events/a-con-versation-with-commandant-of-the-u-s-coast-guard-admiral-paul-f-zukunft); and Niklas Granholm, Marta Carlsson, and Kaan Korkmaz, *The Big Three in the Arctic: China's, Russia's and the United States' Strategies for the New Arctic* (Stockholm, Sweden: FOI, 2016).

20. Defense Science Board, "Task Force on Cyberdeterrence," Department of Defense, Washington, D.C., February 2017 (www .acq.osd.mil/dsb/reports/2010s/DSB-CyberDeterrenceReport_02 -28-17_Final.pdf).

21. North Atlantic Treaty Organization, "Euro-Atlantic Part-nership Council," Brussels, Belgium, April 7, 2016 (www.nato.int /cps/en/natolive/topics_49276.htm).

22. See U.S. Government, "ForeignAssistance.gov," Washing-ton, D.C., 2016 (http://beta.foreignassistance.gov/explore#).

23. U.S. Army Europe, "Army Strong, Strong Europe! Exer-cise Rapid Trident," U.S. Army Europe Headquarters, Weisbaden, Germany, 2016 (www.eur.army.mil/RapidTrident).

24. North Atlantic Treaty Organization, "Relations with Geor-gia," Brussels, Belgium, June 7, 2016 (www.nato.int/cps/en/natohq/ topics_38988.htm); and Ian S. Livingston, Heather L. Messera, and Michael E. O'Hanlon, "Afghanistan Index," Brookings In-stitution, Washington, D.C., February 28, 2011 (www.brookings .edu/wp-content/uploads/2016/07/index20110228.pdf).

25. Stefan Forss and Pekka Holopainen, *Breaking the Nordic De-fense Deadlock* (Carlisle, Pa.: Strategic Studies Institute, U.S. Army War College, 2015), pp. 57–58; and North Atlantic Treaty Organ-ization, "Key NATO and Allied Exercises," Brussels, Belgium, July 2016 (www.nato.int/nato_static_fl2014/assets/pdf/pdf_2016_07 /20160704_1607-factsheet_exercises_en.pdf).

26. For background, see Eoin Micheal McNamara, "Securing the Nordic-Baltic Region," *NATO Review,* 2016 (www.nato.int /docu/Review/2016/Also-in-2016/security-baltic-defense-nato /EN/index.htm).

27. Statista, "U.S. Arms Exports, 2015, by Country," Hamburg, Germany, 2016 (www.statista.com/statistics/248552/us-arms -exports-by-country).

28. See, for example, F. Stephen Larrabee and Peter A. Wilson, "NATO Needs a Southern Strategy," *National Interest* blog, January 27, 2014 (http://nationalinterest.org/commentary/nato-needs -southern-strategy-9769?page=3).

29. On the Syria issue, see, for example, Michael O'Hanlon, "A Trump Strategy to End Syria's Nightmare," *Wall Street Journal,* December 15, 2016 (www.wsj.com/articles/a-trump-strategy-to -end-syrias-nightmare-1481847575); and Michael O'Hanlon, "Deconstructing Syria: A Confederal Approach," Washington, D.C., Brookings Institution, January 2017 (www.brookings.edu/research /deconstructing-syria-a-confederal-approach).

30. Richard C. Bush, *Untying the Knot: Making Peace in the Taiwan Strait* (Brookings Institution Press, 2005), pp. 23–24.

31. Department of State, "Key Facts about the Open Skies Treaty," Washington, D.C., June 2016 (www.state.gov/t/avc/rls/2016 /258061.htm); Daryl Kimball, "The Conventional Armed Forces in Europe (CFE) Treaty and the Adapted CFE Treaty at a Glance," Arms Control Association, Washington, D.C., August 2012 (www .armscontrol.org/factsheet/cfe).

32. David M. Herszenhorn, "Fears Rise as Russian Military Units Pour into Ukraine," *New York Times,* November 12, 2014 (www.nytimes.com/2014/11/13/world/europe/ukraine-russia -military-border-nato.html); and Mark Urban, "How Many Russians Are Fighting in Ukraine?," BBC, March 10, 2015 (www.bbc .com/news/world-europe-31794523).

33. Joe Gould, "Electronic Warfare: What U.S. Army Can Learn from Ukraine," *Defense News,* August 2, 2015 (www.defensenews .com/story/defense/policy-budget/warfare/2015/08/02/us-army -ukraine-russia-electronic-warfare/30913397).

34. Colonel J. B. Vowell, "Maskirovka: From Russia, with Deception," *RealClearDefense,* October 31, 2016 (www.realcleardefense .com/articles/2016/10/31/maskirovka_from_russia_with _deception_110282.html?utm_source=RealClearDefense+Mornin g+Recon&utm_campaign=2db8be085d-EMAIL_CAMPAIGN _2016_10_30&utm_medium=email&utm_term=0_694f73a8dc -2db8be085d-81835773#!).

35. Lucien Kleinjan, "Conventional Arms Control in Europe: Decline, Disarray, and the Need for Reinvention," *Arms Control Today,* vol. 46, no. 5 (June 2016), p. 24.

36. Tim Boersma and Michael E. O'Hanlon, "Why Europe's Energy Policy Has Been a Strategic Success Story," *Order from Chaos* blog, Brookings Institution, Washington, D.C., May 2, 2016 (www.brookings.edu/blog/order-from-chaos/2016/05/02/why -europes-energy-policy-has-been-a-strategic-success-story).

37. Angela E. Stent, *The Limits of Partnership: U.S.-Russian Relations in the Twenty-First Century* (University Press, 2014), pp. 264–65.

38. For one perspective on Russia and Kosovo, see Strobe Talbott, "To Understand Putin, Look to the Past," *Washington Post,* March 21, 2014. For some of Putin's views on missile defense, American conventional force modernization concepts, like prompt global strike, and the broader correlation of forces, see Vladimir Putin, State of the Union speech, December 12, 2013.

39. See James Sherr, *Hard Diplomacy and Soft Coercion: Russia's Influence Abroad* (London: Royal Institute of International Affairs, 2013), p. 57.

40. Dmitry Adamsky, "Defense Innovation in Russia: The Current State and Prospects for Revival," *IGCC Defense Innovation Briefs,* University of California Institute on Global Conflict and Cooperation, January 2014.

Index